D0228487

THE PAST IN PERSPECTIVE

This book is to be returned on or before
the last date stamped below.

REVOLUTION IN AMERICA

TOWER HAMLETS COLLEGE LIBRARY
POPLAR HIGH STREET
LONDON E14 0AF
Tel: 071-538 5888

THE PAST IN PERSPECTIVE

Series Editors: C.C. Eldridge and Ralph A. Griffiths

C.C. Eldridge is Reader in History at St David's University College, Lampeter, University of Wales.

Ralph A. Griffiths is Professor of Medieval History at University College of Swansea, University of Wales.

THE PAST IN PERSPECTIVE

REVOLUTION IN AMERICA

BRITAIN AND THE COLONIES, 1763–1776

Peter D.G. Thomas

CARDIFF
UNIVERSITY OF WALES PRESS
1992

TOWER HAMLETS COLLEGE LIBRARY
POPLAR HIGH STR
LONDON E14 0AF
Tel 071-538 5888

O11062

973.27

© Peter D.G. Thomas, 1992

British Library Cataloguing-in-Publication Data
A catalogue record for this book is available from the British Library.

ISBN 0-7083-1128-8

All rights reserved. No part of this book may be reproduced, stored in a retrieval system, or transmitted, in any form or by any means, electronic, mechanical, photocopying, recording or otherwise, without clearance from the University of Wales Press, 6 Gwennyth Street, Cardiff, CF2 4YD.

Order No:
Class: 973·27 THU
Accession No: 011062
Type: L

─ HAMLETS COLLEGE LIBRARY
POPLAR HIGH STREET
LONDON E14 0AF
Tel: 071-538 5888

Typeset by Alden Multimedia Ltd., Northampton
Printed in Great Britain by Billings Book Plan Ltd., Worcester

Contents

Editors' Foreword

Each volume in this series, *The Past in Perspective*, deals with a major theme of British, European or World history. The aim of the series is to engage the interest of all for whom knowledge of the riches of the world's historical experience is a delight, and in particular to meet the needs of students of history in universities and colleges — and at comparatively modest cost.

Each theme is tackled at sufficient length and in sufficient depth to allow each writer both to advance our understanding of the subject in the light of the most recent research, and to place his or her approach in due perspective. Accordingly, each volume contains a historio-graphical chapter which assesses how interpretations of its theme have developed, and have been criticized, endorsed, modified or discarded. Each volume, too, includes a section of substantial excerpts from key original sources: this reflects the importance of allowing the reader to come to his or her own conclusions about differing interpret-ations, and also the greater accessibility nowadays of original sources in print. Furthermore, in each volume there is a detailed bibliography which not only underpins the writer's own account and analysis, but also enables the reader to pursue the theme, or particular aspects of it, to even greater depth; the explosion of historical writing in the twentieth century makes such guidance invaluable. By these perspec-tives, taken together, each volume is an up-to-date, authoritative and substantial exploration of themes, ancient, medieval and modern, of British, European, American and World significance, after more than a century of the study and teaching of history.

C.C. Eldridge and Ralph A. Griffiths

Explanatory note
References to the Illustrative Documents which follow the main text are indicated by a bold roman numeral preceded by the word 'DOCUMENT', all within square brackets [**DOCUMENT XII**].

Preface

The American Revolution was a complex phenomenon. This brief survey focuses on the basic quarrel about the constitution of the British Empire, tracing the gradual American denial of British sovereignty over the colonies. The documents have been selected to illustrate this theme of the growing clash of opinion between Britain and America. This emphasis has inevitably been at the expense of some kinds of deeper analysis. Thus while attention has been drawn to the circumstance that many individual colonists had cause to cherish grievances against Britain, there has been no exploration of such contentious issues as the role of class conflict within America as a factor in the colonial challenge to British rule. Nor has much heed been paid to interpretations of the Revolution now discarded or downplayed, such as those emphasizing economic oppression or religious apprehension as a key to American resistance.

In a sense this study represents the distillation of twenty-five years of research on and teaching about the American Revolution. I am grateful for much corrective and creative advice from reviewers and students alike during this period. Mr David Jenkins of the University College of Wales Library kindly prepared the map. Nerys Briddon and Wendy Williams cheerfully transformed my horrible holograph into neat typescript.

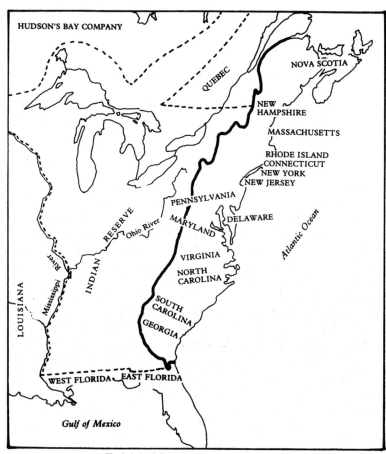

HUDSON'S BAY COMPANY

QUEBEC

NOVA SCOTIA

NEW
HAMPSHIRE

MASSACHUSETTS

RHODE ISLAND
CONNECTICUT
NEW YORK
NEW JERSEY

PENNSYLVANIA

RESERVE

Ohio River

MARYLAND

DELAWARE

INDIAN

VIRGINIA

Atlantic Ocean

NORTH
CAROLINA

River

Mississippi

SOUTH
CAROLINA

LOUISIANA

GEORGIA

WEST FLORIDA   EAST FLORIDA

Gulf of Mexico

British North America in 1763

1. How Historians Have Seen the American Revolution

The American Revolution was the first great modern revolution. Its nature and causes have been subject to varying and sometimes conflicting interpretations, often the result of political and national bias. The classic portrayal for much of the nineteenth century was of a struggle for freedom, as in George Bancroft's massive *History of the United States* (10 vols., 1834–74). That the Revolution was caused by the threat to liberty in both Britain and America posed by the attempted tyranny of George III was for long an axiom of historical faith, evident in such British accounts of the subject as George Otto Trevelyan's *American Revolution* (4 vols., 1899–1913) and that in W.E.H. Lecky's *History of England in the Eighteenth Century* (8 vols., 1878–90). But by the beginning of the twentieth century this simplistic Whiggish interpretation was being challenged by historians who were better informed and more objective in outlook.

There developed in America the so-called 'imperial school of historians', who sought to place the American Revolution in a wider context. The most influential was Charles Mclean Andrews in his brief but seminal *Colonial Background of the American Revolution* (1924). His theme was that the growing political maturity of the American colonies made inevitable a conflict with a mother country determined to maintain its traditional sovereignty. Detailed studies, such as Leonard Woods Labaree's *Royal Government in America* (1930) and Lawrence A. Harper's *The English Navigation Laws* (1939), showed that it was absurd to equate British rule with tyranny. This view has since been spelt out in detail by one of Andrews's pupils, Lawrence Henry Gipson, in his enormous *The British Empire Before the American Revolution 1748–1776* (15 vols., 1936–70). Already prosperous and self-reliant by the 1750s, the colonies resented the British measures that from 1763 sought to put some reality into a sovereignty that had hitherto been largely nominal, and decided to throw off membership of the Empire once it seemed to become burdensome.

Simultaneously with this reinterpretation, there was another by historians who made a detailed examination of events within individual colonies. By analogy with later revolutions in Europe, they produced a picture of the Revolution as motivated by internal class conflict. This 'Progressive' interpretation, as it is known, postulated the theory that the driving force behind the Revolution was less a struggle for home rule from Britain than one over who should rule at home, a view most famously expressed by Carl L. Becker in his *History of Political Parties in the Province of New York, 1760–1776* (1909). The contest with Britain provided the opportunity for the unprivileged to secure democracy in America as well as independence for it. In 1926 J. Franklin Jameson's *The American Revolution Considered as a Social Movement* (1926) equated it with the French Revolution as an alteration of colonial society and a significant advance towards democracy.

By the 1930s, this concept had come to dominate writing on the Revolution, but since 1945 it has faced a formidable challenge, notably by Robert E. Brown and B. Katherine Brown in *Middle-Class Democracy and the Revolution in Massachusetts, 1691–1780* (1955) and in *Virginia, 1705–1786: Democracy or Aristocracy?* (1964). Their portrayal of an extensive franchise for the assemblies in these two colonies led to the broader view that the Revolution was fought to defend democracy in America rather than to attain it. Studies of other colonies also produced evidence of a wide electorate, and a further implicit attack on the Progressive contention that class conflict was the motivation behind the Revolution came with the picture by Jackson T. Main, in his *Social Structure of Revolutionary America* (1965), of colonial America as a land of opportunity and social mobility.

In a sense the argument between Progressive historians and their critics over the extent of colonial democracy has come to seem in recent decades increasingly irrelevant, as detailed studies of individual colonies have demonstrated that a significant feature of American politics during the Revolutionary period was a series of internal struggles for power, not between different classes, but between rival factions within the local power-structures — with the balance of advantage almost invariably falling to the party that challenged British policy most strongly. (Two among several case histories may be studied in David S. Lovejoy, *Rhode Island Politics and the American Revolution, 1760–1776* (1958), and Bernard Mason, *The Road to Independence: The Revolutionary Movement in New York,*

1773–1777 (1966).) But while these writings help to explain the impetus towards revolution, they do not directly explain what the quarrel was about.

Material grievances were not the cause, for twentieth-century historians have explored, and in the main rejected, the notion that economic oppression was a mainspring of the Revolution. This verdict of orthodox economic historians, such as O.M. Dickerson in *The Navigation Acts and the American Revolution* (1951), has been confirmed by practitioners of the New Economic History, who have compared theoretical models of a supposedly independent America with actual knowledge of the eighteenth-century colonies. Their verdict is that British rule inflicted no significant economic burden on America. (On this, see Gary M. Walton, 'The New Economic History and the burden of the Navigation Acts', *Economic History Review* (1971), and sources cited therein.)

Other colonial apprehensions and complaints have been examined and discarded by historians seeking 'the causes of the American Revolution'. Unfounded fears of religious oppression, grievances over the presence of an army, or over enforcement of the trade laws, the belief that Britain intended to prevent westward expansion — such matters contributed to the alienation of many individual colonists from Britain, but do not explain the movement towards independence.

While some historians were playing down materialist motives, others pointed to the intellectual heritage of British concepts of liberty as the seed-bed of revolution, thereby reviving the idea that the colonies had fought for abstract freedom (Max Savelle, *Seeds of Liberty: The Genesis of the American Mind* (1948)). This approach was taken further by Bernard Bailyn in *The Ideological Origins of the American Revolution* (1967), where he demonstrated how the colonists came to regard British policy as a conspiracy designed to deprive them of their liberty.

That was, of course, nonsense. All detailed studies of British policy-making in recent decades have demonstrated how the various ministers of George III acted towards the colonies in what they deemed a properly constitutional manner, but it was a different notion of the imperial structure from that cherished in America (see the studies of British policy in the Bibliography).

It was against this background of political sensitivity in the colonies that British policy initiatives were launched. Modern scholarship tends to stress the genuine nature of American concern over the constitutional implications of the legislation for the colonies being passed by the British Parliament. Edmund S. Morgan and Helen M. Morgan re-emphasized in *The Stamp Act Crisis: Prologue to Revolution* (1953) that American objections were based on the principle of 'no taxation without representation', and, as this present survey seeks to demonstrate, broader constitutional objections developed from that principle. Current interpretations centre once more on the clash over British sovereignty, but the wheel has not turned full circle. Now the root cause is perceived to be the claim of Parliament, as championed by British politicians, not the behaviour of King George III.

2.   Problems of Empire

Why was it that the first successful colonial rebellion in America occurred in the most liberal of the European empires? The question in one sense provides its own answer. The British Empire was never based on military control of settlement colonies, and it therefore lacked the large army that would have been necessary to suppress the resistance that escalated into revolution. That development took place, moreover, because the British colonists had inherited and adapted the political traditions of the home country. The rhetoric of the colonial resistance movement was often couched in language reminiscent of the seventeenth-century conflict between Crown and Parliament, when flight to the New World from Stuart political and religious oppression had been a prime motive of colonization, and remained a folk memory thereafter. In the American Revolution there was the twist that Parliament was now cast in the role of putative tyrant. The colonial quarrel with Britain was over whether Parliament was the supreme legislature of the British Empire.

History and tradition were on the side of the colonists, for Parliament was a belated intruder on the imperial scene. Of the thirteen colonies that were to rebel against Britain, all had had royal charters of foundation and only three, Maryland, Pennsylvania and Delaware, remained in the hands of private proprietors. Their governors, except for those in the proprietary colonies and the two elected in Connecticut and Rhode Island, were appointed by the King, as was the governor of a fourteenth colony to the north, Nova Scotia: formerly the French colony of Acadia and acquired in 1713, this still had a largely French population and did not join in the rebellion.

Orders, instructions and information were dispatched to the colonies in the King's name by his Secretaries of State. The Privy Council, formally 'the King in Council', could make laws for the colonies and still did so, as by the Royal Proclamation of 7 October 1763. The colonies were defended by the King's army and by the royal navy. Their trade was regulated by the King's Customs. Above all, they each had their own elected assemblies, small in membership but with powers of internal legislation and taxation. These mini-Parliaments were deemed by Americans to be equivalent in status under the Crown to the mother Parliament at Westminster.

Yet that Parliament ranked them little higher than the borough corporations in Britain, and, although the Americans might claim to be ruled by the King, the royal framework of empire had long been outmoded in practice. All Britain's colonies, in America and elsewhere, accepted Parliament's regulation of the imperial economic system. It was Parliament which voted the finance for the army and navy that defended them. Policy-making, moreover, lay with politicians who, though appointed by the King, were dependent on Parliament for implementation of their proposals and for their tenure of office.

The course of political evolution in Britain had by now placed the power of deciding measures in the small group of ministers who comprised the cabinet. The unofficial Prime Minister, designated simply 'the Minister', was usually the First Lord of the Treasury, though Chatham in 1766 became merely Lord Privy Seal, a formal post not always in the cabinet. If a commoner, the First Lord was also Chancellor of the Exchequer, a cabinet post in its own right only from 1766. The other members included the Secretaries of State, Northern, Southern, and, from 1768, American; the Lord Chancellor, as head of the law; the Lord President of the Council, chairman of the Privy Council; always the First Lord of the Admiralty, and sometimes the head of the army, such as Lord Granby, its Commander-in-Chief from 1766 to 1770. Departmental responsibility for the colonies, apart from financial business, lay with the Southern Secretaries until January 1768, and thereafter with the American Secretaries. They devised colonial policy for the cabinet, which would then accept, modify or reject their proposals. A specialist department solely concerned with the colonies and commerce was the Board of Trade and Plantations, useful for advice and information, and effectively subsumed within the new American Department from 1768.

The size of the cabinet might be as small as six, when offices were left vacant or held in tandem, and was never above a dozen. The evolution of this small, efficient cabinet was a very recent development, finalized only in 1763 when holders of certain court offices ceased to attend. But it was where power now lay. King George III, aged twenty-five in 1763, was not a man to play a passive role in politics. He would often inform ministers of his opinions, and was indeed sometimes consulted by them; but that was as far as royal influence on policy went. George III acted in accordance with accepted constitutional practice. In the end, he would accept his cabinet's decisions, and at this time he never changed his ministers because he disapproved of what they had done.

Nor did any ministry encounter problems over American policy at Westminster, despite the absence of the modern constraint of party discipline. Sixty years ago, Sir Lewis Namier analysed and described the structure of Parliamentary politics at this time, and for the period of the American Revolution his picture has not been seriously challenged by revisionist historians. The 558 MPs fell broadly into the three groups of independents, politicians, and placemen. Most numerous, sometimes perhaps an overall majority of the House of Commons, were the independents. Some were always opposed to government and others strongly disposed to support it, but many of them, estimated to number about 150 MPs in the 1770s, were open to persuasion. The political battle at Westminster was largely for the hearts and minds of the independents, who held the balance of power if they could be persuaded to attend. All ministerial policies on America received comfortable and often overwhelming Commons majorities, but such support could not be taken for granted. Policies were evidently drafted with Westminster opinion in mind, and often the political temperature would be tested by general resolutions of principle before firm policy proposals were made.

This was the reason for the great importance of the second type of MP, the politicians. Speeches genuinely swayed voting in the House of Commons at this time, and these were the men who made most of them. Many of these politicians, numbering perhaps a quarter of the House, were loosely organized in groups around major figures, such as, in 1763, the Duke of Newcastle, William Pitt, and the Duke of Bedford. Others played a more individual role, but would attract supporters as the result of holding office; George Grenville did when he was Prime Minister from 1763 to 1765. It was essential for every ministry to have a line-up of good debaters, and each was based on one or more political groups. The key figure was the Leader of the House. The Prime Minister would fulfil this role if he were a commoner, and it was no coincidence that the strongest ministries of the period, those of George Grenville and Lord North, were headed by MPs. Administrations headed by peers often encountered problems in the House of Commons, which disliked being ruled by proxy. Such difficulties arose despite the fact that to obtain a

Commons majority any ministry could rely on the block vote of the
third type of MP, office-holders of one kind or another, from army
colonels to sinecurists in the royal Household. The estimated size of
this Court party varies according to definitions and circumstances,
but at this time it may conveniently be put at around 150. The
regularity of attendance of these MPs provided any ministry with a
customary working majority. When added to the politicians in office
and sympathetic independents, these placemen provided a make-
weight in favour of stable government. Any minister chosen by the
King would have a Parliamentary majority in normal circumstances.

The appointment of George Grenville as Prime Minister in April
1763 was a great surprise to contemporaries. Grenville was widely
thought to lack the character and ability for the post, and he certainly
lacked a personal party. But his choice was overshadowed in the
public mind by the surprise decision of George III's favourite, Lord
Bute, to resign. For the political story of the reign since the King's
accession in 1760 had been his determination to have his former tutor
as Premier. This he had accomplished in May 1762, after the resignation over policy clashes of William Pitt and the Duke of Newcastle,
partners in the coalition ministry that had achieved victory in the
Seven Years War against France and her allies. Both then vainly
opposed the generous terms of the Peace of Paris by which Bute's
ministry had ended the war. Bute's administration came to an end
simply because he decided that politics was not his *métier*, and the
King, determined not to surrender to the Parliamentary opposition,
pressed Grenville into service.

Grenville had initially been in Bute's cabinet as Northern Secretary
and Leader of the Commons, but failure in the latter capacity led to
his replacement by Henry Fox, and demotion to the Admiralty. He
was nevertheless the only man whom George III could call upon
when Fox insisted on retiring at the same time as Bute. With the
prestige and patronage of being head of the ministry, Grenville now
proved a success in the Commons, establishing his mastery early in
1764. From the autumn of 1763 he also enjoyed the full confidence of
his sovereign, who at first had caused a crisis by privately consulting
Bute. The Bedford party formed an integral part of the administration, with the Duke as President of the Council and Lord Sandwich
as Northern Secretary. American matters were in the capable hands
of Lord Halifax, immensely knowledgeable after thirteen years as

President of the Board of Trade. That post was now held by the competent Lord Hillsborough. It was an able and experienced ministry, politically secure in both Court and Parliament, that would consider the problems of empire at the end of the Seven Years' War.

In 1763 Britain entered an era of unwonted European peace. It was time to take stock of the empire, new and old. Problems existed all over the world: close at hand in Ireland, where direct British control was to be restored in the 1770s; far away in India, where Lord North's Regulating Act of 1773 was a bold and successful decision to introduce Crown officials into the government of the extensive and populous new territories under the East India Company; additional possessions had been acquired in 1763 in the West Indies and in West Africa. But the main focus of attention was to be on North America.

Here Britain now ruled the entire continent east of the Mississippi River. By the Peace of Paris, France ceded to Britain Quebec and all lands north and south of the Great Lakes up to that river, while Spain gave up Florida. These areas contained about 100,000 Frenchmen, 5,000 Spaniards and some 250,000 Red Indians. Britain already held the Hudson Bay territories in the north, Newfoundland and Nova Scotia to the east of Quebec, and the thirteen old settlement colonies along the Atlantic coast from New Hampshire to Georgia, with a population estimated at already over two million. Although much attention was naturally focused at first on the new territories, American policy was to be primarily concerned with the older colonies. Their defiance of the trade laws had long been notorious in Britain, and their growing political maturity was a cause for alarm among the British officials and politicians who knew about such matters. Astute observers, indeed, had already anticipated that problems of imperial control would now be increased by the removal of the French threat from Canada.

There was much to be decided concerning America in 1763, and the attention accorded the colonies by the Grenville ministry has caused some historians to postulate the idea of 'a Grenville programme'. The matter was rather one of devising solutions for problems new and old — a task any administration would have had to undertake — and, in any case, the American measures sprang from diverse antecedents. Some had already been decided in principle before Grenville became Prime Minister, such as the restriction of westward settlement, and the retention of an army in North America to be financed by a colonial tax. Taken together, the policies adopted by government during the next few years conveyed to Americans the impression of a tightening of control over their affairs by Britain, and in various ways caused resentment towards the home country. Yet the significance of such issues should be viewed in perspective. Grievances over western settlement restrictions, colonial currency regulations, the trade laws, and billeting of the army all contributed to colonial discontent but, although alienating many individuals, they should not be confused with the underlying cause of the American Revolution. The break between Britain and America occurred over the conflict of ideas about their constitutional relationship, in comparison with which all other issues fade into minor complaints. Yet for much of the decade from 1763 these issues formed a background to the main controversy.

In studies of the American Revolution, much attention has been given to the western frontier question. Initial arrangements for the government of the new territories were made by the end of 1763. Fear of alienating the Red Indians by encroaching on their lands and a realization that inland colonies would develop political and economic independence were the chief motives behind the principle of a western boundary beyond which settlement should not be allowed. In July the Grenville cabinet adopted a Board of Trade suggestion that this should be the mountain watershed between the coastal plain and the Mississippi Valley. That vast area, much of it a forest wilderness, was to be left to the Indians, and defended by army forts. There already existed two Indian Superintendents, entrusted with the unenviable task of protecting the Indian tribes from unauthorized settlers and unscrupulous traders, and they were now given the duty of establishing an actual boundary on the ground to accord with the line drawn on maps in Whitehall. North and south of this Indian reserve, three new colonies were created for the areas where white settlers already lived: Quebec for the French inhabitants of the St Lawrence Valley, and East and West Florida for the sparse Spanish population along the southern coast (see map on page x). These new colonies, unlike the older ones, were not to have elected assemblies until they contained more British settlers. News of an Indian rebellion, the Pontiac Rising, injected a sense of urgency into the decision-making process, and on 4 October the Privy Council approved a Royal Proclamation embodying these plans. It was promulgated by George III three days later. [**DOCUMENT I**]

During the next few years, the unexpectedly large cost incurred in maintaining both an Indian Department — for the Superintendents headed an organization of commissaries, interpreters and other officials — and a military presence in the forest wilderness led to proposals for economy, notably through the withdrawal of most of the army garrisons. But Lord Shelburne, when Southern Secretary from 1766 to 1768, had other ideas, and in 1767 he even proposed three new colonies in the area between the Great Lakes and the Ohio River. There were many Americans — land speculators, humble settlers, and merchants — who favoured such western plans, but their hopes were temporarily dashed by the accession of Lord Hillsborough to office as American Secretary in 1768. He was a rabid anti-expansionist, his view being that further settlement should instead be encouraged in the thinly populated coastal colonies of Nova Scotia, Georgia, and the Floridas. General Gage, commander of the army in North America, was accordingly encouraged to call in as many of his far-flung garrisons as he deemed wise. Yet Hillsborough was to be thwarted in his aim of blocking westward expansion, initially by Northern Indian Superintendent, Sir William Johnson, who in 1768 concluded Indian treaties for a settlement line well to the west of what had been intended in 1763. The indignant American Secretary discovered that his ministerial colleagues were inclined to favour western settlement, and were unconcerned about the financial and military implications. Four years later, Hillsborough resigned when overruled in his opposition to a plan to create a new colony of Vandalia in the Ohio Valley — with the subsequent irony that legal problems prevented its establishment after all.

The often-made assumption that British government policy was against western settlement, and therefore contributed significantly to the break with the colonies, is an obvious misinterpretation. Although Britain began in 1763 with a firm policy of prohibiting westward settlement, even then that was avowedly temporary [**DOCUMENT I**], and within a few years Hillsborough was evidently fighting a lone and vain battle to maintain it. The year 1772 clearly saw the abandonment of the idea as official policy. As a practical grievance, it had never had much substance, since individual settlements over the mountains had proved impossible to check. In any case, although the 'western lands' issue may have been a grievance in the minds of some Americans, those leading the break with Britain were not concerned with events on the remote frontier.

The acquisition of the new territories entailed the maintenance of an army of substantial size, both for defence and for control of areas populated by foreigners and Indians. After the first year, the size of the army was to be 7,500 men, and not the 10,000 often stated; even so, the average annual cost was £385,000. The Bute ministry had already decided that the expense of this army should be borne by the colonists, but it had not decided how the money should be raised.

This question soon became entangled with the overhaul of the trade laws, and especially an attempt to remedy the most famous breach of them, the evasion of a 1733 act imposing a duty of 6*d*. a gallon on molasses from the foreign West Indies. Molasses is a sugar product from which was made the popular colonial drink of rum. By Grenville's American Duties Act of 1764, popularly known as the 'Sugar Act', this duty was halved to 3*d*., and the prospective revenue from it allocated towards payment of the army costs in America. This was a failure. Widespread smuggling continued and, instead of the anticipated revenue of £60,000, the duty yielded only £5,000 in 1764 and £4,000 in 1765. The Rockingham ministry in 1766 therefore reduced it to 1*d*. a gallon, low enough to discourage evasion, and, after offering to the British West Indies concessions on inter-island trade, imposed it on British as well as foreign molasses. That change eliminated widespread fraud, and meant the conversion of the molasses duty from a trade regulation to a simple tax. It proved to be the only effective tax on America devised by British politicians during the revolutionary period, and soon produced the equivalent of about 10 per cent of the army costs. During all the furore over taxation that sparked off the clash with Britain, the colonists paid the molasses duty, despite its obvious similarity to Charles Townshend's import duties which were furiously objected to after their imposition in 1767.

Americans presumably paid the molasses duty because of confusion arising from its origin as a trade regulation. Parliament in the seventeenth century had imposed on the British Empire a protectionist system of trade laws, the Navigation Acts, which were continually being refined and updated. The prime motives were to exploit the colonies as a market for British goods and as a source of products needed in Britain, such as rice, sugar and tobacco. Care was also taken to foster colonial economies, and modern scholarly opinion is that the adverse effect on colonial life was minimal. The colonists professed to accept this regulatory power of Parliament in theory, however much it was resented and evaded in practice. Grenville in 1763 made great efforts to enforce the trade laws, threatening absentee customs officials with dismissal and encouraging the navy to play an active role; and his American Duties Acts of 1764 and 1765 included many provisions for the improvement and enactment of trade regulations. Throughout the next decade, other ministers continued the war against smuggling. Charles Townshend in 1767 created a separate American Customs Board at Boston, and on several occasions in the 1760s different ministers sought to use the Admiralty courts to secure convictions of smugglers, for those courts sat without juries.

Even during the lull in the political storm that occurred during the early 1770s, enforcement of the trade laws proved a running sore in the Anglo-American relationship. American politicians might pay lip-service to Parliament's right to regulate commerce, but colonial merchants resented interference with their accustomed free-trading practices. Bribery and coercion of customs officials were widespread, and violent incidents common. Despite all the evidence the government possessed about defiance of the trade laws, it took no action until the naval schooner *Gaspée* was burnt on 10 June 1772 after going aground when in pursuit of Rhode Island smugglers. A Commission of Inquiry was instituted of four American lawyers chaired by the Rhode Island Governor, with authority to send suspects to Britain for trial. But a local conspiracy of silence frustrated the investigation, and there was an ominous colonial response — the creation, on the initiative of Virginia, of a network of Committees of Correspondence of the various assemblies. British authority had been further discredited; a potential resistance organization had been created throughout the colonies, and American suspicion of Britain intensified. Altogether, the *Gaspée* incident was a political disaster for the government. The trade laws, both ineffective and provocative, contributed greatly to ill-feeling between Britain and America.

So did two specific measures passed by the Grenville ministry, the Currency Act of 1764 and the Quartering Act of 1765: each led to grievances lasting for nearly a decade. It had long been the practice of colonial assemblies to issue paper money, dated to last for a specified number of years, but this had led to the use of depreciated money for the payment of colonial debts to British merchant creditors, especially by Virginia. That colony had already been warned to mend its ways, and its failure to do so caused Hillsborough's Board of Trade on 9 February 1764 to make an official report suggesting that there should be a ban on all future issue of paper money as legal tender, since the practice was fraudulent and unjust. Action was initiated, not by the ministry but by a back-bench MP, American merchant Anthony Bacon, who on 4 April proposed to prohibit the legal use of all paper money. Alarmed colonial agents — official representatives of the colonies in London appointed by the assemblies — thereupon persuaded the ministry to modify this suggestion to accord with the Board of Trade proposal. Existing paper money would then continue as legal tender, even though no more such currency could be issued. That was the basis of the Currency Act, which therefore had little immediate impact on colonial life. But within a few years, as existing currency issues expired, complaints over the inconvenient shortage of legal currency began to flow into Whitehall. Nothing was done while Lord Hillsborough was American Secretary, for he was a critic of paper money. After his resignation in 1772, a partial solution was effected, based on the widespread practice by colonial treasuries of accepting paper money for payment of taxes and other public debts. Parliament in 1773 passed an act to legitimize this habit by making paper money legal tender in such transactions, but private creditors, such as British merchants, were still under no obligation to accept it.

If this grievance had been resolved before the final decision for rebellion, so also in effect had been that over the billeting of soldiers. The Grenville ministry had had no thoughts of a Quartering Act until a request came from General Gage, who had been encountering colonial obstruction over the quartering of his troops. When Gage's report arrived on 1 March 1765, the War Office suggested that soldiers should be billeted in private houses where there were insufficient barracks or taverns. George III and Grenville vetoed that idea, fearing a Parliamentary storm over such an infringement of 'liberty'. The solution devised by Grenville in the Quartering Act was that soldiers should be billeted in uninhabited buildings, such as public halls, barns, and empty houses. This, however, necessitated a further clause stipulating that such troops should be provided, free of charge, with fuel, candles, bedding, cooking utensils and alcohol by the local colony's assembly. That requirement became a grievance. The colonists had a double cause for complaint in this provisions clause; it was seen not only as a new tax, but as one that was unfair, since its incidence was accidental. Some colonies escaped altogether. Others found it a heavy burden, notably New York. Refusal by that colony to pay in 1765 and 1766 led to direct coercive action in 1767: the proposed closure of the assembly by Act of Parliament. This legislation never came into operation, for the assembly coincidentally gave way at the very same time, but the Quartering Act remained an intermittent colonial grievance for some years. Hillsborough, when American Secretary, hit upon a practical solution in 1771, namely, the withdrawal of army units from recalcitrant colonies. This prompted a realization that the economic and military benefits of an army presence outweighed the financial burden. Apart from the special case of turbulent Massachusetts, the problem of the Quartering Act had virtually been solved before the final confrontation between America and Britain.

During the decade after 1763, the American colonists thought they had numerous grounds for complaint against Britain, and the more so since various measures could be construed as an overall scheme for closer British control of, or interference in, the colonial way of life. But while many Americans had individual cause for concern at the apparent trend of British policy, the clash over Parliamentary sovereignty was centred on one theme, the attempt by Parliament to levy taxes on the colonies. There did in fact exist a procedure by which the Crown could call upon them for financial contributions, when the King directly required assemblies to provide money for specific purposes, usually their own defence. This so-called 'requisitions system' had never worked satisfactorily. Colonies had been reluctant to pay even at the height of recent wars in America. British politicians therefore brushed aside suggestions for its revival. Nor did colonists seriously propose it or any other method as an alternative to Parliamentary taxation. Since they also rejected any idea of representation at Westminster, it is difficult to avoid the conclusion that the fine slogan 'no taxation without representation' was in reality a selfish cry of 'no taxation'.

Taxation was to be the anvil on which the Anglo-American relationship broke. Other, practical, grievances could be solved, fudged or evaded. But the clash of constitutional principle involved in the dispute over Parliament's claim to sovereignty escalated from one crisis to another, as the point of dispute widened from internal taxation to all taxation to all legislation, before the final challenge came to the authority of the Crown itself.

3.   Crisis One: The Stamp Act

The Stamp Act Crisis began even before the passage of the Stamp Act in 1765. Prime Minister George Grenville at first intended to introduce it in 1764, and the measure formed part of his Budget Day proposals on 9 March of that year. The Treasury had been preparing an American Stamp Bill since September 1763. Stamp duties had been levied in Britain since the seventeenth century, and by this time produced a net revenue of over £250,000. They were imposed on newspapers and much other printed matter for public sale, on property conveyances and a whole range of other legal documents, on cargo lists for ships, and on such sundry other items as playing-cards and dice. Their extension to the colonies had often been suggested in recent decades. During the Commons debate of 9 March, Grenville agreed to postpone the taxation, accepting suggestions that the colonies ought first to be informed and consulted; at a subsequent meeting with colonial agents on 17 May, he even hinted that he might be willing to listen to ideas for alternative Parliamentary taxes, but would not agree to the colonies taxing themselves.

No colony put forward any such alternative. Instead protests against the proposed Stamp Act were made by the assemblies of at least eight colonies. None acknowledged Parliament's right of taxation or authorized its agent to consent to the Stamp Bill. Four agents deputed to meet Grenville on 2 February 1765 could therefore only propose the discredited system of requisitions, but by that date Grenville's determination to impose a Parliamentary tax had been reinforced by knowledge of the colonial objections. On 9 February Treasury Secretary Thomas Whately wrote to an American correspondent to make this point:

> The great measure of the session is the American Stamp Act. I give it the appelation of a great measure on account of the important point it establishes, the right of Parliament to lay an internal tax on the colonies. We wonder here that it was ever doubted. There is not a single Member of Parliament that will dispute it.[1]

That letter was written three days after the main debate on the stamp duties. Grenville, when introducing the taxation on 6 February, argued that the logic of the American stance was a complete challenge to the authority of Parliament, although the colonists were not in fact to adopt that view for nearly a decade: 'The objection of the colonies is from the general right of mankind not to be taxed but by their representatives. This goes to all laws in general.' It was only equitable that America should pay something towards its own defence costs, Grenville said, concluding with the reminder that the colonies had not produced any alternative suggestion. [**DOCUMENT II**] In the ensuing debate, no MP challenged Parliament's right to tax America, although William Beckford, a West Indies planter and merchant, warned that the Americans distinguished between internal taxes and such external ones as the molasses duty levied the previous year. A dozen speakers opposed the tax on grounds of inexpediency and folly, but the Ministry won the day by 245 votes to 49. After this test of Parliamentary opinion, critics of the tax confined themselves to desultory sniping, and did not force another vote. During the passage of the Bill, the ministry developed the theme that Parliament was the supreme legislature for the entire empire under the Crown, and that argument was thereafter to be the cornerstone of the British case to tax and legislate for America.

The Grenville ministry did not proceed with the Stamp Act in ignorance of American opinion, but thought the measure would be accepted under protest, and took care to avoid all reasonable objections. The total tax burden envisaged was small, the Treasury forecast being a revenue of £100,000. This, even with £50,000 from the molasses duty, would not cover half the £350,000 estimated as the annual cost of the army in America. Over fifty duties were imposed, on the same basis as in Britain; this wide range had been chosen to ensure an equitable distribution of the burden, and many were lower than in Britain, none higher. To meet two other possible complaints, the Grenville ministry arranged that the money would be paid directly to the army in America, thereby ensuring that there would be no drain of specie, and it further decided that the Act would be administered by colonists, not by British officials. There was keen competition for the key post of Stamp Distributor in each colony, for it would provide income, patronage, and prestige. Some Americans in London obtained these appointments for themselves, others, including Benjamin Franklin, for friends in America. No one in the early summer of 1765 anticipated violent resistance to the Stamp Act.

For reasons quite unconnected with America, the Grenville ministry was dismissed from office by George III in July 1765. The motive was simply the King's dislike of the Prime Minister. After William Pitt declined to form a new administration, George III turned to the Duke of Newcastle's party, now headed by the young Marquess of Rockingham. He took office with the Duke of Grafton and General Henry Conway as Northern and Southern Secretaries of State. Conway was nominally Leader of the House of Commons also, but the ministry's strong man there was William Dowdeswell, a country squire who had been a surprise choice as Chancellor of the Exchequer. It was a ministry deemed to lack not only experience but also ability; yet Rockingham and Dowdeswell rose to the challenge better than anticipated, and Rockingham's new secretary, Edmund Burke, proved to be a superb Parliamentary orator.

The change of ministry did not necessarily imply a change of American policy, for little opposition had been made by these men to Grenville's measures. Nevertheless, it was important that at the time of the Stamp Act Crisis there was in power an administration which had not been responsible for the taxation that provoked the colonial discontent, and which was willing to solve the problem by conciliation. Grenville would not have sought to do so if still Prime Minister.

News of the Stamp Act reached America in April. The initial reaction was despair, not defiance, and Lieutenant-Governor Thomas Hutchinson of Massachusetts was one official who expected that the measure, though unpopular, would be accepted. None of the assemblies made any response until 29 May. The Virginia House of Burgesses was only one-third full when Patrick Henry won instant fame with his Resolves. Four of his resolutions were voted, asserting the doctrine of no taxation without representation. The significance of the Virginia Resolves was the misleading publicity afforded them in the colonial press, which printed not four but seven resolves, including a declaration of disobedience to Parliamentary taxation even though the assembly had not endorsed such a stand.

The mood of America changed. When the assemblies met again later in the year, that of Rhode Island in September voted all that Virginia was thought to have done. Other assemblies, perhaps better informed, did not go so far, but by the end of 1765 at least seven more had voted declaratory resolutions. One of these, Massachusetts, had in June merely voted respectful petitions to King and Parliament, but it had also circulated other colonies with the suggestion of a meeting of delegates to organize a joint petition to the King. Nine colonies sent a total of twenty-seven representatives to what has since become known as the Stamp Act Congress, which met in New York during October. Only one, New Hampshire, declined to do so, but three others were prevented from attending when their governors refused to summon assemblies. The Congress voted a petition to George III, and did more besides. The delegates had no doubt that the Stamp Act was unconstitutional, and formed resolutions accordingly. Allegiance to the Crown and subordination to Parliament were acknowledged in general terms, but the claim was made that only their assemblies had the power to tax them. The Congress did not even concede Parliament's right to regulate colonial trade, for the Sugar Act had shown how trade duties could be used to raise revenue. [**DOCUMENT III**] This refusal to admit Parliament's right in any way to raise money from the colonies was not clearly understood in Britain, where the general impression prevailed that the colonies would not in fact object to such 'external taxes'.

Deeds of resistance reinforced these words of protest. The Stamp Act was prevented from coming into operation on its due date, 1 November, by intimidation of the Stamp Distributors. The resignation of the Massachusetts official was brought about by violence on 14 August, and a similar riot in Rhode Island caused the resignation of that colony's Stamp Distributor at the end of the same month. After these events, the mere threat of violence sufficed elsewhere. By 1 November there was not one official willing to enforce the stamp duties in the thirteen colonies; but in Georgia the only non-American appointed did act for some weeks after his very belated arrival on 4 January 1766.

The colonists continued to engage in most of the relevant activity, for to refrain from doing so would have been a tacit admission of the Stamp Act's validity. They soon opened their ports. Virginia did so after one day, and by February 1766 ports in all thirteen colonies were open and trading illegally. The lawyers were more cautious than the merchants. They lacked immediate commercial pressures, and decisions recorded on unstamped papers might be invalid. There is no clear picture or consistent pattern concerning the response of the legal profession, but it would seem that in most colonies there was a slow resumption of normal business. The printers, together with the merchants and lawyers, formed the third occupational group whose livelihood was directly affected by the Stamp Act. The colonial press had played a key role in promoting American resistance to it, both by propaganda and simply by reporting words and deeds of defiance; but most newspapers adopted the cautious response of suspending publication. Only eight out of twenty-three continued to publish without a break; within a few weeks others gradually resumed publication, and the majority were soon defying the law.

This widespread initial hesitation reflected colonial awareness of the enormity of the challenge being made to Britain; yet the recent American experience of rebuffs to pleas and petitions made resistance appear to be the sole available method of altering Parliament's attitude. However, even refusal to pay the tax and resumption of taxable activities would produce only a stalemate. Petitions needed to be backed by pressure on Britain itself. The method adopted was a boycott of British goods. Since the Stamp Act Congress had confined itself to verbal remonstrances, the boycott was instigated by individual ports. New York led the way on 31 October, Philadelphia followed on 14 November, and Boston on 9 December. Elsewhere British orders were usually cancelled without formal port agreements. This boycott would be significant more for its threat than for its impact, which was necessarily limited in the time-scale involved; in any case, only one-eighth of Britain's total exports went to America. An exaggerated effect on British opinion was produced, however, by the coincidence of the colonial boycott with an existing commercial and industrial recession in Britain. The Rockingham ministry misunderstood the situation by assuming that it was caused by the colonial trade embargo.

News of the American resistance to the Stamp Act gradually reached Britain during the second half of 1765. The Rockingham ministry tacitly postponed any policy decision until December, hoping that the crisis would resolve itself. By then the cabinet could no longer expect that the Stamp Act would come into operation after the colonial storm had blown itself out. Some form of conciliation was inevitable, for ministers knew that it would be impossible to enforce the taxation in the face of such hostility. Their dilemma was that any concession would be unacceptable to British political opinion, because it would seem too obviously to be a surrender to mob violence.

It was resolved by the attitude of William Pitt, the dominant figure in Parliament. On 14 January 1766 he attended the House of Commons after a two-year absence, and spoke in favour of complete repeal of the Stamp Act. Adopting what was generally thought in Britain to be the colonial view, Pitt denied that Parliament had any right to levy internal taxation on America, since the colonies were not represented at Westminster. [**DOCUMENT IV**] The Rockingham ministry thereupon knew that it would be possible to implement the compromise policy already being devised in government circles. This would comprise two parts, one a Declaratory Act asserting the right of Parliament to legislate for the colonies 'in all cases whatsoever'. [**DOCUMENT V**] That was an expression of political faith, an integral part of future Rockinghamite attitudes to America. But there was also the motive of tactical expediency. It was the sugar to persuade King, Lords and Commons to swallow the bitter pill of the repeal of the Stamp Act. That was the other part of the ministerial policy, ostensibly introduced on the grounds of the legislation's inherent faults and the detrimental effect it had had on the British economy.

The ministry faced opposition on both measures. Pitt's denial of the right of taxation would cause him to challenge the Declaratory Bill. In the event, he did not force a vote in the Commons, and his followers lost by 125 to 5 in the Lords. The passage of repeal was a harder battle, despite a carefully planned ministerial campaign. A battery of twenty-four petitions from British ports and manufacturing towns, and the examination of twenty-six witnesses by the House of Commons, provided a wealth of evidence on the economic woes of Britain, attributed of course to the loss of American trade. MPs, moreover, were led to believe that the colonists challenged Parliament only over internal taxation, and also that the colonial disturbances were merely spontaneous riots, not organized violence. Nevertheless, Grenville was at first so confident that he could block repeal that on 7 February he proposed enforcement of the Stamp Act. Royal support for the ministry and fears of bloodshed in America produced a majority against him of 274 to 134.

The great debate on repeal took place on 21 February. It was significant for the public statement of the various British opinions on America. Conway expounded the Rockinghamite line when he said that Parliament's undoubted right of taxation ought not to be exercised at the expense of British trade. Pitt put forward what was to be his interpretation of the colonial relationship, that it was unfair both to tax America and to control her economy. Grenville argued in vain that America should and could pay his taxes. The resolution for repeal was carried by 275 to 167. Independent opinion in Parliament was overwhelmingly behind the ministry on this issue, for fear of the consequences in Britain and America. Both measures received the royal assent on 18 March. The policy achieved the desired aim in

America, though not in Britain where recovery from the economic recession took some years. The colonial boycott of British goods ended, and economic and political relationships returned to normal, at least on the surface; underneath things could never be the same again.

Although the Stamp Act Crisis was concerned ostensibly with the issue of taxation, it had raised the wider question of Britain's sovereignty over the colonies, and had consequences on both sides of the Atlantic. British opinion was not satisfied with the formal claim of the Declaratory Act, and there remained a strong popular demand for a colonial revenue. In Britain, politicians were now categorized according to their attitudes on America. Henceforth, Grenville, Bedford and their friends were deemed hardliners or 'Stamp Men'. The Rockinghamite party, the largest single political group, would be pragmatic in approach, championing Parliamentary sovereignty in theory but not its exercise in practice. Sympathizers with America were few in number — mostly Pitt and his followers, and a handful of radicals — and certainly not in full accord with colonial views. In America the colonists would now regard any British government policy with suspicion, and in some colonies the controversy had a considerable impact on local power structures. Politicians identified with support of Britain, such as Thomas Hutchinson in Massachusetts, found their influence weakened or destroyed; while championship of America had brought new men to prominence, notably Patrick Henry. Neither in general nor in detail would the Anglo-American relationship again be what it had been before the Stamp Act Crisis.

4.   Crisis Two: The Townshend Duties

Rockingham's American policy was generally deemed a success in resolving the colonial problem. Although George III was among those who later thought repeal of the Stamp Act the fatal concession that opened the floodgates of revolution in the colonies, such a consideration formed no part of his motives in dismissing Rockingham as Prime Minister in July 1766. The King had for several months nurtured doubts about the competence of his administration, and some years earlier had identified Pitt as the man who could fulfil his political ideals by constructing a government of talent — individuals chosen for ability and integrity rather than influence and connection. Pitt had now declared his willingness to do so. But his ministry, despite high hopes and brave words, was to be narrowly based on his own personal followers and a few Rockinghamites, and proved a disastrous mix of incompatible personalities. Pitt himself threw away its chief prospective asset, his dominance of the House of Commons, by accepting a peerage as Lord Chatham and, moreover, took only the non-executive post of Lord Privy Seal. The Treasury went to the Duke of Grafton, who had left Rockingham's cabinet in May. Lord Shelburne became Southern Secretary, with responsibility for America, but a more significant appointment for the colonies was to be that of the brilliant, forceful, erratic Charles Townshend as Chancellor of the Exchequer. Conway was the only Rockinghamite to remain in cabinet office, as Northern Secretary and Leader of the Commons, the others being alienated by Chatham's dictatorial behaviour. The Bedford group refused office because of past differences of opinion over America, and no offer was made to Grenville. The plan of a broad-based ministry of talent was stillborn. Instead, the Chatham administration faced a formidable opposition of three parties headed by Rockingham, Grenville and Bedford.

On America this was not to matter. There was no clear line of battle, such as might have been anticipated from the events of the Stamp Act Crisis, between an opposition that championed Britain's full sovereignty over the colonies and a ministry with other ideas. Although the politicians who had opposed the Declaratory Act were now in office, they fully accepted its implications. Contrary to both contemporary expectation and historical tradition, the Chatham ministry reasserted Parliamentary supremacy over the colonies, and the resumption of American taxation formed part of that policy from the outset. This attitude was not inconsistent with what Chatham (as Mr Pitt) had said earlier in 1766. He had then declared that he would support strong measures if conciliation failed to produce quiet in the colonies, and he had condemned only 'internal taxation' of America by Parliament. Chatham soon lapsed into ill health and played no constructive part in the formulation of policy, but the measures of the ministry he had created were in accordance with his earlier opinions. Townshend's use of customs duties to raise revenue exploited what was thought by Chatham and most other politicians to be American acquiescence in 'external taxation'. Nor was Townshend's action that of the lone headstrong individual of legend. Soon after the Chatham ministry took office, the search for a colonial revenue began. The cabinet was divided not over whether to tax America, but only over how best to do so. Shelburne favoured the idea of annual quit-rents from land granted for settlement, but by March 1767 information arriving in Whitehall showed that this was not a feasible source of revenue. Before the end of 1766 ministerial opinion was already coming to favour the idea of customs duties, and on 18 February 1767 Townshend informed the House of Commons that he proposed to adopt the colonial distinction of internal and external taxes, even though he himself thought it nonsense.

In April, before making specific proposals, Townshend altered the aim of the proposed taxation. It was not to be used towards army costs in America, the purpose of the earlier colonial taxes. Instead he resurrected an old idea of his from the 1750s, that of freeing the administration of government in America from financial dependence on the colonial assemblies, by paying the salaries of governors, judges and other officials out of his new taxes. This was to make the new measure doubly alarming to Americans, as it seemed to threaten the *raison d'être* of their assemblies.

Townshend's ideas on what to tax were numerous and varied. Salt, foreign wine and citrus fruits were originally on his agenda, but dropped after mercantile protests. The most important item on his final list, announced on 1 June, was tea, to be taxed at 3*d.* a lb. to yield £20,000 a year. The same sum would be produced by his other import duties, on china, glass, paint and paper. The total anticipated revenue of £40,000 was criticized by Grenville and others as derisory, but that was to misunderstand Townshend's aims. They were political rather than financial — the re-establishment of the practice of colonial taxation and the making of Parliamentary provision for the cost of civil government in America. No significant opposition was made to the passage of what has become known as the Townshend Duties Act, and it is easy to see why. The taxation of America was in response to a popular demand for revenge and revenue. The colonists were not thought to object in principle. The Rockinghamite party did not regard the duties as onerous, while Grenville merely thought them inadequate.

Before the American storm broke, the ministry was reconstructed. Townshend died suddenly on 4 September. The accession to office of his successor, Lord North, can be seen as a metamorphosis of the political scene. North was the main prop of government for the next fifteen years, Leader of the Commons from early 1768, and Prime Minister from 1770 to 1782. Charming and intelligent, he was in other respects the antithesis of Townshend. North, dependable and conscientious, proved to be the minister George III had been seeking since his accession, for he combined financial and administrative expertise with Parliamentary skills of a high order. Grafton, deputizing for Chatham, had already sought to strengthen a ministry much buffeted in Parliament the previous session, when the easy passage of American taxation proved the exception. In July a negotiation with Rockingham had failed, with important implications for the future of American policy-making. All the portents were that a ministry based on the Chatham and Rockingham factions would have proved more conciliatory than the one based on the Bedford and Grenville groups that came into existence under Lord North. For at the beginning of the next session, in November 1767, continued quarrelling over America between Grenville and the Rockinghamites caused the Bedfordites to despair of opposition prospects. They joined the Chatham ministry at the end of 1767, Gower becoming President of the Council, and Weymouth Northern Secretary in place of Conway, who remained in the cabinet without office. Grafton took the opportunity of the reshuffle to create a new post of Secretary for America. His choice fell on Lord Hillsborough, twice President of the Board of Trade earlier: his would be a stronger hand at the helm of colonial policy.

Whereas the Stamp Act Crisis had erupted promptly and universally throughout the colonies, American resistance to the Townshend duties was a plant of slow growth. No Congress of colonial delegates met, and no effective trade boycott developed for nearly two years. But complaints at public meetings and in the colonial press were widespread before the end of 1767. The most significant protest was the publication in Philadelphia newspapers of the 'Letters of a Pennsylvania Farmer', written by local lawyer John Dickinson. He explicitly challenged the right of Parliament to levy any taxes whatsoever, internal or external, on the colonies; but he did concede Parliament's right to regulate colonial trade and industry. [DOCUMENT VI] The 'Farmer's Letters' were widely reprinted and endorsed by public meetings throughout the colonies. This unequivocal denial of any Parliamentary right of taxation was a clear escalation of the conflict of opinion between Britain and America.

The Massachusetts Assembly put forward the same doctrine in a Circular Letter of 11 February 1768 to other assemblies. This, like Dickinson, conceded that Parliament was 'the supreme legislative power over the whole empire', but claimed that taxation by the Townshend duties was an infringement of the rights of American subjects because they were not represented in Parliament. News of this circular brought an immediate riposte from the ministry. The American Secretary, Lord Hillsborough, counter-circularized all American governors on 21 April, instructing them to prevent any replies from their assemblies; and the next day Massachusetts Governor Francis Bernard was ordered to obtain a retraction from his assembly, on threat of dissolution. A few weeks later, on 8 June, Hillsborough ordered the dispatch of soldiers and naval ships to Boston, to enforce the trade laws there. This was in response to the pleas of local customs officers and, although the move increased political tension in the port, it did not initiate the confrontation that now ensued. Massachusetts was already in an uproar, and violence occurred in Boston on 10 June, when a mob resisted the efforts of customs officials to impound for smuggling the ship *Liberty*, owned by John Hancock, a wealthy merchant and prominent local politician. In this heated atmosphere, the Massachusetts Assembly rejected by 92 votes to 17 the ministerial demand for the withdrawal of its Circular Letter: few of the small minority retained their seats at the next assembly election.

The other colonies were already rallying to the cause of resistance. Eight had made a positive response before news came of Hillsborough's circular, and the other four did so before the end of 1768.

By then all thirteen colonies had sent petitions or addresses to the King, deliberately ignoring Parliament, although some also sent complaints to Westminster. The invariable reply of governors to the protest movement had been, under instructions from London, to prorogue or dissolve the assemblies. It was probably this firm stand that prevented the summoning of another Congress, and left any practical retaliation, as in 1765, in the hands of the merchants: for the experience of the Stamp Act Crisis had convinced the colonists that a trade boycott would change ministerial policy.

Nothing much was achieved in this respect during 1768. Philadelphia refused to endorse a Boston initiative for a general ban on imports from Britain, and New York thereupon withdrew its assent to the proposal. Boston nevertheless decided on 1 August to suspend such imports from 1 January 1769, and New York then voted a similar ban, to begin two months earlier. But other ports failed to follow this lead, Philadelphia insisting on awaiting news of the reception of the petitions sent to Britain.

This failure to organize a trade boycott coincided with the collapse of Boston's defiance. On news of the *Liberty* riot, the ministry on 27 July ordered the dispatch of more soldiers to the town. There followed a period of tension in London, where many expected an armed confrontation. But when news reached Boston in September of the imminent arrival of a thousand soldiers, prudence prevailed over passion. Two regiments quietly disembarked there at the end of the month, the guns of their naval escort being trained on the town. This bloodless coup was to cause British politicians to regard Bostonians as blusterers whose bluff could be called — an opinion that proved erroneous six years later.

For the moment, the sequence of events made it possible for Grafton to propose conciliation from a position of strength. There were formidable political difficulties at home in the way of such a policy. Numerous reports were going back to America about the widespread anger in Britain at the colonial defiance and violence, and of the desire for retribution against Massachusetts. Yet Hillsborough and other ministers now perceived that, apart from tea, Townshend's duties were a discouragement to the home economy because they were levied on the exports of British manufactured goods. A genuine economic argument could therefore be added to that of political expediency for doing something to allay the colonial discontent.

Before the time came for policy-making there occurred another ministerial change. Chatham, who had taken no part in political decisions for about eighteen months, finally resigned as Lord Privy Seal in October 1768 on grounds of ill health. Shelburne, already at odds with his colleagues on personal as well as political grounds, left with him, to be succeeded as Southern Secretary by a professional diplomat, Lord Rochford. Grafton was now Prime Minister in name as he had long been in practice; but on America opinion in his cabinet was to prove finely balanced. There were four Chathamites left, Grafton, Lord Chancellor Camden, and the two armed forces ministers, Lord Granby as head of the army and Sir Edward Hawke at the Admiralty. Together with former Rockinghamite Conway, they would be for conciliation. But the other five cabinet members were hardliners — the two Bedfordites, Gower and Weymouth, and Hillsborough, North, and Rochford.

This political balance in the cabinet meant that ministerial policy on America would be neither the coercion nor the complete repeal of taxation that represented positive alternatives. Instead the decision was to wave a big stick before offering concessions. Retributive action would be threatened against Massachusetts, and consideration then given to redress of American grievances. As in the Stamp Act Crisis, this was a compromise intended to solve the double problem of British indignation and colonial defiance. The ministry therefore intended to propose a series of Parliamentary resolutions condemning the recent behaviour of the Massachusetts Assembly and Boston town. This would be followed by an Address to the effect that the Boston rioters should be prosecuted in Britain under a treason law of Henry VIII. The cabinet also decided that there could be no repeal of the Townshend duties in the Parliamentary session of 1768–9. Some ministers wished to do more, to alter the Massachusetts charter and to arrest the Boston ringleaders; the failure to exact proper retribution was certainly to astonish friend and foe in America. Grafton prevailed in his opinion that provocative action was best avoided, at a time when news of the quiet occupation of Boston was accompanied by reports of the widespread refusal of colonies to join the trade boycott. The Duke hoped that implicit acceptance of British authority by America — or what could be construed as such — would make future concessions possible: it was unofficially leaked that what was being contemplated was repeal of Townshend's duties in the following session of 1769–70.

It was a difficult line of policy to follow. After Grenville perceptively denounced the Parliamentary resolutions as 'waste paper', pressure mounted early in 1769 for positive initiatives. Hillsborough responded to demands for tougher measures with a miscellaneous group of suggestions that included alteration of the Massachusetts Charter. His colleagues rejected them all. Friends of America were also dissatisfied, unwilling to wait until 1770 for redress of grievances. On 19 April, MP Thomas Pownall, a governor of Massachusetts in the 1750s, proposed that the House of Commons should take the Townshend Duties Act into consideration. He was acting independently of both opposition and administration. Although the debate ended inconclusively, it proved a useful sounding-board for ministers. Enough was said for them to know that there would be strong support for some concession next year.

The cabinet came to its decision on 1 May 1769. There were by now additional arguments in favour of repeal: the knowledge that the Townshend duties had yielded only £11,000 in the first fifteen months, and news that Philadelphia was preparing to join the trade boycott. News of future concessions might prevent intensification of the embargo on British goods, and at least it would divide colonial opinion. The policy decision was whether to repeal all the duties, or to retain the tea tax. The latter brought in three-quarters of the revenue, sufficient to fulfil much of the original purpose of paying the salaries of colonial officials. The tax on tea, moreover, was not liable to the argument for the removal of the other duties on home manufactured goods, namely, that they were detrimental to the British economy. Grafton, with the political aim of conciliation, nevertheless proposed for 1770 the repeal of all the duties. That had certainly been the expectation held out during the previous winter. But he was outvoted by five to four over retention of the tea duty, Hawke among his potential allies being absent. [**DOCUMENT VII**] The concession to the colonies was therefore a token one, removal only of the other duties that had been insignificant in their revenue yield. This fateful decision was to prove the point of no return in the sequence of events leading to the American Revolution. Without a tea duty there would have been no Boston Tea Party and no consequent final quarrel between Britain and her colonies.

This cabinet decision was officially communicated to the colonies. Before news of it arrived in America, the assemblies of Virginia and Massachusetts had voted resolutions that were a deliberate retort to those of Parliament. Nor when the ministerial policy was known did it act as a deterrent to the boycott. Boston scornfully rejected the compromise. Many American merchants, especially in the southern colonies, were reluctant, however, to implement the decisions voted by politicians. British exports to America in 1769 fell by only 38 per cent as compared with 1768. The American market, moreover, represented only 16 per cent of Britain's total export trade. The overall impact of the colonial boycott on the British economy was therefore small, overshadowed by fluctuations in trade elsewhere. There was not enough distress to cause complaint, and the ministry successfully discouraged petitions from merchants and manufacturers. The American boycott had no practical effect on British policy.

It was not to be Grafton who enacted that policy. The political portents for his ministry became ominous in the summer of 1769. Already the Rockingham and Grenville parties had allied over the Middlesex Elections case during the previous session. That was one of the most famous political controversies of the century, the denial to John Wilkes on personal grounds of the Parliamentary seat to which he was elected four times. Many MPs not opposed to the administration were uneasy and alarmed at the possible implications of the decision, and it proved to be the issue over which the Grafton ministry was toppled. Chatham now allied with Grenville and Rockingham when he at last recovered from his ill health in July. Grafton was faced with the prospect of a truly formidable Parliamentary opposition, headed by three former Prime Ministers, each leading a party — a unique phenomenon in British politics. The end came when Parliament met in January 1770. Immediate Chathamite defections from the cabinet included Camden and Granby. Conway followed when Grafton himself resigned on 26 January, his nerve having broken when his Commons majority tumbled from 96 to 44.

George III's government was on the point of collapse, but the King was saved from having to surrender to the opposition by the willingness of Lord North to take the lead. The amiable North was popular as well as competent. On 31 January he secured a majority of forty when many had predicted his defeat, and after a hard Parliamentary battle he was safe by the end of February. With the political crisis over, his ministry could consider America. The cabinet had now shed all four members who had favoured repeal of the tea duty in May 1769, and still contained all five of the majority for keeping it. Since none of the vacancies was filled, and with Hawke lax in his attendance, what had been a close decision became a unanimous ministerial opinion, and on 5 March the House of Commons was asked to confirm it.

North, aware that many MPs would dislike any concessions at all, began with a vigorous denunciation of colonial behaviour. The

Americans had not responded to last summer's promise of relief. Their boycott was illegal, but would soon collapse. Having thus established that what he was going to propose should not be seen as a climb-down, North declared that anger should not overrule reason. The duties imposed on British manufactures were detrimental to the export trade and should be removed: but there was no reason to repeal the tea duty. Tea was a luxury, and not a British product. The tax, though light, was remunerative, and would go a long way towards paying the costs of government in America, Charles Townshend's original purpose, which North now endorsed. The repeal of the other duties might not satisfy colonial opinion, he said, but the American distinction between revenue duties and duties for the regulation of trade was one that would lead to endless argument.

William Beckford began the attack, voicing the Chathamite view that Britain should be content with a monopoly of colonial trade. Thomas Pownall moved an amendment to include the tea duty, which was also uncommercial, he claimed, because it encouraged smuggling. Grenville and his followers could support neither the motion nor this alteration, since each involved concessions to defiant colonists, and they were to walk out before the vote. Conway argued for repeal of the tea duty; some administration supporters argued against any repeal at all. The Rockinghamite spokesmen, William Dowdeswell and Edmund Burke, did not speak in the debate, but their party voted in the minority when Pownall's amendment was defeated by 204 votes to 142. [**DOCUMENT VIII**] There was little more Parliamentary discussion before the measure received the royal assent on 12 April.

That the American trade boycott would now collapse was the obvious hope of the North ministry. That hope was realized, despite the unfortunate coincidence, also on 5 March, of the Boston Massacre. The military occupation of Boston was then nearly eighteen months old, and showed no signs of ending. What happened in Boston was not a spontaneous clash, but a contrived confrontation, the motive either a mobbish desire for a fight or a deliberate plot to create a situation in which it would be impossible to refuse a local demand for the removal of the army. A small group of soldiers under attack with sticks and stones opened fire and killed five men. An indignant town meeting secured the immediate withdrawal of the garrison to Castle William, an island fort in Boston Bay. The incident at first threatened to alienate colonial opinion, but a reaction soon set in as moderate men had their eyes opened as to what might lie ahead on the path of resistance to Britain. The Boston Massacre became irrelevant to colonial opinion over the trade boycott.

The effective decision was made by the three major ports of Boston, New York and Philadelphia. In Boston the mercantile community was intimidated by mass meetings manipulated by radical politicians, but in the other two ports the international merchants were more free to take their own decisions. It was soon apparent that outside Massachusetts the ministerial tactic of partial repeal had sown dissension. On 14 May the Philadelphia merchants suggested that the boycott should be lifted except on tea. A hastily convened Boston town meeting countered on 23 May by voting to continue the boycott until the tea duty was repealed. But the Philadelphia proposal was an attractive one for ports where virtually all the tea imported had been smuggled from Holland, and New York's merchants decided to adopt it. On 9 July they took a unilateral decision to that effect, after sounding public opinion in a town where many were suffering economic hardship.

For a while it seemed as if New York might be alone. Even Philadelphia merchants condemned the desertion of 'the cause of liberty'. Virginia had renewed its boycott on 22 June, and Newport, Rhode Island, did so in August. But merchants elsewhere could not allow New York to engross American trade, and Boston itself was widely suspected of cheating. Philadelphia decided to adopt the New York agreement on 20 September. Boston followed on 11 October, and as the news spread boycotts elsewhere gradually collapsed, often without any formal decisions. This sequence of events left a legacy of mutual antipathy that would render difficult future colonial co-operation.

At the end of 1770 the North ministry's American policy appeared to be a triumphant success, and many must have thought the colonial crisis solved. There occurred at the same time another ministerial reshuffle that made any relaxation of policy even less likely. Caused primarily by the death of Grenville in November, it completed a polarization of British politicians on America. Within a few weeks Grenville's more important followers joined the ministry. Lord Suffolk became Northern Secretary, and Alexander Wedderburn Solicitor-General, while Bedfordite Sandwich replaced at the Admiralty the last surviving Chathamite in the cabinet, Sir Edward Hawke. The 'Stamp Men' were in office, the self-styled friends of America in opposition and powerless to influence policy-making in the crucial period ahead. Chatham now virtually withdrew from politics for some years, while the Rockinghamites were a dwindling and disheartened faction. Even when the mild Dartmouth succeeded Hillsborough as American Secretary in 1772, no change of colonial policy ensued. Although Dartmouth's role as President of the Board of Trade in the Rockingham ministry made his appointment welcome in American eyes, his chief motive in taking office was merely to support his stepbrother Lord North, not to launch a policy initiative. The accidents of British politics had put in power in the 1770s a ministry which was hardline on the issue of America.

In retrospect, it might seem as if the British government missed a last opportunity to avert the American Revolution. Such an interpretation is based on the assumption that British politicians would have been prepared to concede what America was demanding — an unrealistic view in the light both of general British assumptions of the subordinate colonial role in the Empire, and of the apparent success of the compromise policy of 1770. Further conciliation was not needed, so it would seem. North's policy was therefore what he had announced to Parliament, the payment of Crown salaries to officials and judges in America as far and as fast as the tea duty revenue permitted. Revenue was available for this purpose, for although the colonial decision to end the boycott of British goods had specifically excluded duted tea, only Philadelphia and New York fully carried out this undertaking. In 1771, for example, Boston and the southern colonies imported 525,000 lb. of taxed tea. Implementation of the Townshend policy had begun in 1768, with salaries for the Massachusetts Chief Justice and New York's Attorney-General. In 1770, it was extended to the Governor of New York, and to the Governor of Massachusetts, now Thomas Hutchinson, and his Lieutenant-Governor. By 1772, with a decision to pay Crown salaries to the other four judges and to the two law-officers in Massachusetts, implementation of the Townshend Duties Act was completed in that colony.

An irony of the situation was that this attempted solution to the problem of control of the colonies was not only provocative but irrelevant. Although an obvious idea to men steeped in recent British history, when Parliament had used the power of the purse to good effect against the Crown, it provided no answer to the practical problem of physical control. In any case, the assemblies had seldom used this weapon against governors, and American concern was defensive — fears, groundless but real, over the implicit threat to the very existence of the assemblies if they were not needed for finance.

Only part of the American complaint against the Townshend

Duties Act concerned payment of colonial officials from the revenue. The older grievance of Parliamentary taxation was more significant, and the colonists never lost sight of this issue after 1770. The British attempts to seek a colonial revenue in the 1760s had initiated an ongoing debate in America about the constitutional structure of the British Empire. The highlight of this was a public controversy early in 1773 between the Governor and Assembly of Massachusetts, with Hutchinson asserting that 'no line can be drawn between the supreme authority of Parliament and the total independence of the colonies'.[1] This challenge unwisely drove the assembly to abandon the previous American distinction between taxation and legislation, a further step towards denial of Parliament's authority altogether. This stance in turn provoked the North ministry into considering at this time legislation that would have anticipated the measures adopted after the Boston Tea Party, but pressure of other business prevented the cabinet from embarking on further American policies before that event precipitated a final crisis.

5. Crisis Three: The Boston Tea Party

The Boston Tea Party began the sequence of events that ended in the Declaration of Independence. It was caused by a circumstance totally unconnected with British policy towards America — the financial crisis of the East India Company. A sharp and unexpected rise in military and administrative expenditure in India had coincided with a fall in commercial revenue, 90 per cent of which was derived from the sale of tea. The fall in the American market was only a minor factor in the steady growth of the Company's tea mountain. Sales in Britain dropped from 7,500,000 lb. in 1772 to little over 4,000,000 lb. in 1773, when the tea in the Company's warehouses amounted to 21,000,000 lb. Tea held in store deteriorated in quality and value, and capital was being tied up by the retention of large stocks. Although the lost American market was one obvious outlet for the surplus, the East India Company looked first to Europe as a better potential market. But realization dawned that tea exported cheaply to Europe would be promptly smuggled back to Britain and would ruin the home market, and the Company turned to America for an outlet.

Although Lord North at once made it clear that he would not remove the Townshend duty, concessions over tea exports to America formed part of the rescue package for the Company devised by his ministry early in 1773. The government's price was Lord North's India Regulating Act, whereby the ministry appointed a Governor-General, officials and judges for India. In return, the Company received a financial loan, and, in a Tea Act, concessions that would enable it to fix a tea price for the American market. A 10 per cent duty levied in Britain was removed, and the Company was now permitted to sell direct to colonial buyers instead of, as hitherto, indirectly through British and American merchants trading with the colonies. By the end of July, the Company had worked out its price strategy. In 1773 smugglers were buying tea in Holland for 1s. 9d. a lb. and selling it in America for 2s. 7d. The Company therefore proposed to sell in America at 2s. a lb., including the 3d. Townshend tax — a price smugglers would find it impossible to match. During August the Company decided to send 600,000 lb. as a first instalment, to four American ports, Boston, Charleston, New York, and Philadelphia.

Neither the North ministry nor the East India Company anticipated difficulty in the implementation of the Tea Act. That attitude was not as foolish as the universal American resistance, only highlighted by the Boston Tea Party, would make it appear in retrospect. The sale of taxed tea to the colonies had never ceased. Boston and Charleston had always imported significant quantities, and a trickle had found its way even into the two smuggling centres of New York and Philadelphia. The lack of foresight was twofold: failure to anticipate a hostile reaction from merchants who would suffer from the new arrangement, and failure to appreciate the continuing colonial resentment at Parliamentary taxation. Unless they could obtain appointment as consignees for the East India Company, the merchants hitherto involved as middlemen in the legal tea trade would face ruin equally with the smugglers, although it was the latter who raised the initial outcry.

The merchants of New York and Philadephia at once portrayed the whole project as a ministerial scheme to trick Americans into acceptance of taxed tea. Popular feeling was aroused by press propaganda and mass meetings in both towns. By the end of November, their tea consignees had resigned, and it was evident that the Company tea would not be sold in either port. Both had already decided to return the taxed tea to Britain even before news reached them of the Boston Tea Party.

Boston had been slower to respond to the Tea Act, and for a while the Massachusetts Governor, Thomas Hutchinson, believed that the port would welcome Company tea at a price much lower than that prevalent, since there was a scarcity at the end of 1773. There would, after all, be little break with existing practice, for the Boston merchants who were appointed tea consignees were those who had been importing dutied tea regularly since 1770. Boston's radicals, headed by merchant John Hancock and journalist Sam Adams, soon, however, raised the issue of rejecting taxed tea. But the course of events in Boston thereafter differed from that in Philadelphia and New York. Popular pressure failed to coerce the tea consignees into resigning. Instead they took refuge in Castle William, the island fort off Boston garrisoned by the British army. The impasse developed into a crisis when the first tea-ship docked on 28 November, soon to be followed by two more. There came into operation a twenty-day customs deadline for the landing of dutiable goods. The possibility existed that the consignees, safe from mob violence, might pay the duty and release the tea for legal sale. Local market conditions and the customs laws caused Boston's political leadership to see no alternative to direct action. A series of mass meetings culminated on 16 December in the Boston Tea Party, just before the expiry of the customs time-limit. Within four hours some 90,000 lb. of tea were thrown into Boston harbour by men tokenly disguised as Red Indians. [**DOCUMENT IX**] This precaution of anonymity was to frustrate the British government's initial plan of immediate retaliation against the perpetrators of a violence that was too obviously a deliberate tactic, not a spontaneous outburst of rage.

In the other colonies the Tea Party was greeted with public jubilation, but much private disquiet. New York heard of it on 21 December. It so happened that no confrontation occurred there, for the tea-ship destined for that port was caught in an Atlantic storm and driven on to the West Indies. The Boston news reached Philadelphia on 24 December, coincidentally the day its tea-ship arrived. That vessel, accepting the decision of a town meeting, left four days later without docking. In Charleston the tea-ship arrived on 2 December. Although some merchants contended that the East India Company had as much right to sell taxed tea as the individuals who had previously done so, a public meeting adopted the defiant stance of the other ports. But, as in Boston and for the same reason, customs officials prevented the departure of the vessel, and Governor William Bull achieved the minor coup of landing the tea and putting it in store, informing the North ministry that it could have been sold but for the timidity of the tea consignees.

No revisionist interpretation of the American Revolution has attempted to discount the significance of the Boston Tea Party as the actual catalyst of the sequence of events whereby the colonies moved from resistance to revolution. It was an open challenge to British authority such as had not occurred in earlier disputes over taxation. The event shocked British public opinion, opposition politicians like Chatham and Rockingham being equally as appalled as supporters of the government. Benjamin Franklin reported back to Massachusetts in March that 'we never had since we were a people, so few friends in Britain. The violent destruction of the tea seems to have united all parties here against our province.'[1]

News of the Tea Party reached London on 19 January 1774, and the Philadelphia tea-ship returned six days later. By 29 January the North ministry knew of the failure to sell the Company tea at all of the three ports at which it had arrived, and of the resistance intended at New York. Yet on 4 February the cabinet decided to take immediate action only against Boston, adopting three proposals of the American Secretary, Lord Dartmouth, for direct executive action. These were to close Boston harbour, to seek punishment of the individuals responsible, and to remove the Massachusetts seat of government from Boston. This was a moderate approach, both in minimizing the sense of confrontation by the avoidance of Parliamentary legislation, and in confining retribution to the scene of actual violence.

It soon proved to be impractical to enact this policy. The government lawyers reported on 11 February that there was insufficient evidence to secure the conviction of any individuals involved in the Tea Party. The cabinet, moreover, had second thoughts about undue reliance on the royal prerogative, and made the fateful decision to proceed through Parliamentary legislation rather than by direct administrative action. For on 19 February it adopted a proposal by Dartmouth to close Boston harbour by Act of Parliament until the town paid financial compensation to the East India Company for the tea. The cabinet also took an even more controversial decision, that of altering the constitution of Massachusetts.

During the previous decade there had been a growing belief among British politicians that it was the constitution of Massachusetts, as established under its charter of 1691, that made the colony so ungovernable. Whereas in the other royal colonies the Council was nominated by the Crown, in Massachusetts it was chosen annually by the Assembly, and from 1766 opponents of the British government had exploited this law to omit supporters of the Governor. As a result, the Council had failed to endorse his proposals for firm action in times of trouble, as before and after the Tea Party. Other democratic features of the Massachusetts constitution included the circumstance that a public meeting was the governing body in each town, and a judicial system of elected juries and magistrates. The latter made almost impossible the conviction of those who defied unpopular British laws, and now seemed to jeopardize any prospects of fair trials for soldiers and officials accused of misdeeds. The legislation of 1774 sought to solve these problems. By 10 March, when the cabinet reviewed its American measures, a Massachusetts Government Bill was envisaged that would alter the method of appointing the Council and magistrates; also planned was a vague measure to provide judicial safeguards for the army, the outline of what was to become the

Massachusetts Justice Bill. This resort to legislation significantly raised the stakes at issue in the dispute with America. Any colonial resistance would now be an overt challenge to the authority of Parliament.

Although the ministry knew that resistance to taxed tea had been general throughout the colonies, its policy was deliberately limited to problems arising from the behaviour of Boston. Recent experience had conditioned British politicians to regard Boston as the centre of American defiance, for it had been the scene of the most notorious violence: the Stamp Act riots of 1765; the *Liberty* riot of 1768; the Boston Massacre of 1770; and now the Tea Party of 1773. But to exasperation there was added the calculation that if that troublesome seat of sedition could be crushed in isolation, the opposition to Britain elsewhere would subside. The colonists were to display a sound political instinct in perceiving Boston to be the first line of defence of their 'liberty'.

Ministerial policy-making remained a well-kept secret, and not until 7 March did the administration bring the American question before Parliament. Government spokesmen made no attempt to play down the crisis, declaring that the question at issue was whether or not the American colonies belonged to Britain, and arguing that their retention was essential to Britain's role as a Great Power, on the mercantilist ground that without political control the advantage of colonial trade could not be assured. Pleas for unanimity did not deter debate. Although the Rockinghamite party condemned American behaviour, they were opposed to the deployment of force against the colonies. Their Commons spokesman, William Dowdeswell, said so, and blamed the ministry for not having repealed the tea duty in 1770 or 1773.

Since nothing was known about ministerial intentions on America, the announcement of the Boston Port Bill to the House of Commons on 14 March proved a great shock. When Lord North sat down, the House was quiet for several minutes. MPs were stunned into silence. In a desultory discussion the measure met with little criticism, though Dowdeswell pointed out that the innocent would be punished along with the guilty, and asked why other ports escaped scot-free. Chathamite spokesman Barré then caused astonishment by expressing warm support for the proposal. No vote was forced on the Boston Port Bill in either House of Parliament, and the ministry secured its passage before the Easter recess at the end of the month. **[DOCUMENT X]** The only long debate took place at the Committee stage on 23 March, when opposition MP Rose Fuller vainly tried to substitute the alternative punishment of a £25,000 fine. 'Would to God it was the first offence!' exclaimed Lord North when rejecting that argument by Fuller. It was in this Committee that backbencher Charles Van made the fiery speech that became notorious in America as supposedly characteristic of British attitudes. The Port Bill, he declared, was quite inadequate. Boston ought to be razed to the ground. 'Make it a mark that shall never be restored. Demolish it. That is my opinion.'[2] Throughout the final American crisis there were always to be MPs who denounced ministerial policy as being too soft on the colonists.

Supporters and opponents of the administration alike accepted that the Boston Port Act was only the first part of the official policy for America. Further revelations of ministerial measures were awaited before genuine debate could commence. To allow MPs consideration of the Massachusetts Government Bill during the Easter recess, Lord North announced it on 28 March, after having anticipated one line of criticism by asserting that Parliament had the power to overrule royal charters. He outlined the defects of the colony's constitution, as he saw them, and the ministry's remedial plans, nomination of the Council and magistrates, and restriction of town meetings to official business. Lord George Germain, a prominent MP then moving over from opposition to support of government on America, suggested also an end to elective juries, and North thanked him for the idea. This curious incident was contrived, many suspected, so as to spare the ministry the odium of attacking a jury system, that renowned buttress of British liberty.

While MPs were digesting these proposals, the ministry completed arrangements for the physical control of Massachusetts. General Gage, commander of the army in America but then home on leave, was appointed temporary governor of the colony. He was instructed to make Salem the colony's seat of government when the Boston Port Act came into effect on 1 June. Gage sailed on 16 April, with four regiments of soldiers; he arrived at Boston on 13 May.

The duration of his voyage virtually coincided with the passage of the Massachusetts legislation. On 15 April North both introduced the Government Bill and announced the Justice Bill. The latter would be a temporary expedient for three years only. In order to secure impartial trials for all concerned in the support of government, soldiers and officials alike, it authorized the governor at his discretion to transfer the trials of such men for capital offences to another colony or, as a last resort, to London. Barré promptly warned that such a provocative measure would convert resistance into rebellion, and the colonists were quick to dub it 'the Murder Act', claiming soldiers could now kill Americans with impunity.

North stated that this was the last measure he would propose, disappointing expectations that as in 1766 and 1770 ministerial policy would combine concession with firmness. There had certainly been some speculation at Westminster that the coercion of Boston would be accompanied by the repeal of the tea duty, with Dartmouth believed to favour that idea. It was now apparent that the opposition would have to take the initiative in the direction of conciliation. It came not from the Chathamite or Rockinghamite leadership but from Rose Fuller, who on 19 April moved for a Committee to consider the tea duty. The administration opposed on the ground that throughout the last decade British concessions had always led to new colonial demands. This debate was the occasion of Edmund Burke's famous 'Speech on American Taxation', but under the cloak of its splendid oratory nothing new was suggested. Burke merely repeated the Rockinghamite view that Britain should abandon the practice of taxing the colonies. Fuller's motion was rejected by 182 votes to 49. The British government in 1774 refused to make any concession to America.

During the subsequent passage of the Massachusetts legislation, the Secretary at War, Lord Barrington, moved for a new Quartering Bill, to obviate difficulties encountered in the 1765 Quartering Act. The aim was to place authority for billeting soldiers in a colony's governor, so that the soldiers could be put promptly into taverns and uninhabited buildings. Contrary to much contemporary and historical misapprehension, there was no intention of placing soldiers in private houses. By mutual agreement between administration and opposition, Parliamentary proceedings were expedited by a decision to hold one major set-piece debate on the Massachusetts legislation, on 2 May. Opposition speakers expressed concern over the absence of safeguards against arbitrary rule, claiming that the Government Bill would drive the colonists into rebellion and the Justice Bill then authorize their slaughter. Such extravagant language was scorned by ministerial speakers, and North had a majority of 239 votes to 64. Throughout the Parliamentary debates on America, government supporters claimed and opposition members admitted that popular opinion was strongly behind official policy, Fuller lamenting on 6 May that 'it is not an error of the ministry, it is an error of the nation. I see it wherever I go. People are of opinion that these measures ought to be carried into execution.'[3]

North repeatedly denied that the American legislation of 1774 comprised a coherent programme, and one can see why. The Boston Port Act involved short-term coercion, to compel that town to obedience and recompense. The Massachusetts Justice Act was a temporary expedient, and the Quartering Act merely a minor modification of an earlier law. Only the Massachusetts Government Act was intended to effect a permanent change. But so, too, was another measure passed after these so-called 'Intolerable Acts', and often associated with them, the Quebec Act; certainly there was much in it that gave offence and alarm to the older British colonies.

For a decade successive ministries had considered the problems posed by the acquisition of a territory on the St Lawrence River containing a French Catholic population of some 100,000 and about 1,000 British settlers. The Board of Trade under both the Grenville and Rockingham ministries had accepted the legality of Catholic worship, then forbidden in Britain itself, and recommended the use of French civil law, two ideas that were to be included in the Quebec Act. Thereafter nothing was done until legislative proposals were formulated by the government lawyers in 1773. They agreed on combining French civil law with English criminal law, and went further than mere toleration by making financial provision for the Catholic Church. But the idea of an elected assembly, such as existed in the older colonies, was rejected, since one based on the small British minority would be inequitable and one of mixed British Protestants and Canadian Catholics a dangerous experiment. Any legislation would have to be by a nominated Council, revenue being provided by import duties on alcohol voted by Parliament. Despite the distractions of the American crisis, a Bill was drafted on these lines, and it also included provisions for restoring the colony's boundaries to the extent claimed by France before 1763, incorporating the western wilderness down to the Ohio River. This momentous decision transformed the Quebec Bill into a dual-purpose measure, designed not merely to settle the internal problems of that colony but also to solve the question of 'the west' that had perplexed and divided British politicians since 1763. Some form of government would thereby be provided for a vast area too often a refuge for rogues; while in the aftermath of the Tea Party, there was developing in Britain a groundswell of opinion that further inland settlements ought to be prevented, since they would be difficult to control.

The Quebec Bill, introduced into Parliament during May, offered several tempting targets for critics: the absence of an assembly; the establishment of a Catholic Church; the retention of French civil law; and the boundary clause. English settlers, it was claimed, were being deprived of their constitutional rights. Opponents of the Bill were vociferous and pertinacious but few in number, mustering only twenty-nine votes against the second reading. But there was much that would arouse concern and anger in the older British colonies. It was now official British policy, announced by North himself among others, that inland colonization was to be discouraged, and the boundary clause both symbolically and literally seemed to embody a British intention of curbing American development. Any favours to Catholics were anathema to the Protestants of nearby New England. French law was popularly associated with tyranny. The creation of a colony without an assembly could and would be construed as an indication of British intentions for other colonies. The American fears were fanned by knowledge of Parliamentary criticism, as when Barré on 7 June talked about the creation in Quebec of a Catholic army. The Quebec Act became another American grievance, and its repeal one of the colonial demands.

Simultaneously with the formulation and subsequent enactment of British policy, events in Boston provided first a spur and then a retrospective justification for the decisions made in London. Knowledge of the refusal of the Massachusetts Council to punish those involved in the Tea Party provided a final motive for the Government Act; the Council declined to offer a reward for information, and decided that any prosecutions should be conducted before an elected jury, composed of the popular leaders themselves. During the early months of 1774, Boston remained under mob rule, and friends of government were intimidated. Threats of violence compelled the judges to revert from Crown salaries to payment by the Assembly. The tea consignees dared not leave their military refuge, and until sufficient soldiers arrived Governor Hutchinson could see no prospect of challenging the control of men like Sam Adams and John Hancock. His replacement, General Gage, who landed well ahead of his regiments, found the Assembly defiant, refusing even to discuss compensation for the Tea Party, and he wrote to American Secretary Dartmouth on 5 July of 'the usurpation and tyranny established here by edicts of town meetings enforced by mobs, by assuming the sole use and power of the press, and influencing the pulpits; by nomination and intimidation of juries and in some instances threatening the judges'.⁴ The arrival of his soldiers enabled Gage to recover control of Boston from July onwards, but the rest of the colony was ruled by the popular party. Gage moved the seat of government back to Boston from Salem on 30 August, and began to put the town into a state of defence. He dared not send out soldiers to maintain a semblance of order elsewhere lest they be overpowered by sheer numbers, and he reported in despair on 2 September that 'civil government is near its end'.⁵

Outside Massachusetts, although many Americans had been shocked by the violence in Boston, colonial opinion was reunited by news of the British retaliation. But the much-publicized role of Boston as the first martyr of American liberty did not lead to the response that that town sought. As soon as news of the Port Act arrived there in mid-May, a town meeting called for a complete trade boycott of Britain and her West Indies. The other colonies showed little inclination to adopt such an immediate retaliation. New York and Philadelphia were unwilling to close their ports. Colonial opinion instead came to favour the summoning of a Congress of delegates to consider what collective response should be made. American attitudes were complex and even contradictory. While some colonists welcomed a Congress as a more moderate alternative to a prompt trade boycott, others of more radical bent thought it a path to colonial unity, and there were conservatives who therefore refused to participate.

Even the New England neighbours of Massachusetts opted for a Congress rather than a boycott. Rhode Island and Connecticut Assemblies adopted that idea in June, and support came also from New Hampshire, which had refused to attend the Stamp Act Congress. New York and Pennsylvania Assemblies, although both under the control of conservative politicians, were compelled by popular pressure to appoint delegates for a Congress which, it was soon agreed, would meet at Philadelphia in September. The formal initiative was a circular letter from Virginia.

The movement for a Congress became almost universal. Georgia alone of the future thirteen rebel colonies declined to attend what would be known as the Continental Congress. When governors prevented the choice of delegations by their Assemblies, unofficial Conventions would take the decision instead, and this circumstance provided the Congress with an unusually broad base of popular support. Local town or county meetings chose representatives for the Conventions, which in turn selected colonial delegations for the

Congress. At least 7,000 colonists publicly identified themselves as resistance leaders through membership of county committees and colonial Conventions. These meetings not only demonstrated widespread support for the forthcoming Congress: they also pre-empted its policy decisions, for 61 of 108 local meetings favoured some form of trade boycott. The majority of delegates were in effect mandated to support at least a non-importation agreement, and there had been little support for the alternative conservative view that the colonies should resort only to petitioning. Most Americans believed that it had been the previous trade boycotts that had secured the repeal of the Stamp Act in 1766 and of most of the Townshend duties in 1770. The Boston predicament imparted urgency to the situation. Something positive had to be done, instead of relying on a British goodwill which had hitherto been lacking. In this atmosphere American supporters of the imperial status quo, the future Loyalists, suffered from the apparent pusillanimity of advocating a policy of virtual inaction, that of mere petitioning. Many now chose to opt out of the controversy, even when called upon to serve in Conventions or the Congress. At all levels, national, provincial, and local, such passivity played into the hands of those intent on challenging Britain.

Colonial defiance had escalated from a mere denial of Parliament's right of taxation — and even the Tea Party had signified only that — to a complete challenge to Parliament's right of legislation for the colonies. This reaction was widespread, being either overt or implicit in the resolutions of many county meetings and colonial Conventions demanding repeal of the 1774 measures. The constitutional stance of the Congress, as well as the practical retaliation of a trade boycott, had already been widely anticipated.

When the Continental Congress began at Philadelphia on 5 September, the debate would not be on whether to challenge the 1774 legislation, but merely on the best method of doing so, by remonstrance alone or by a trade embargo. That argument was soon over. Joseph Galloway, the leader of the Pennsylvania delegation, had been hoping to form a party strong enough to prevent a boycott, but he soon found that a majority of southern delegates, as well as those from New England, so strongly favoured that measure that opposition from the more conservative middle colonies of Pennsylvania, New York and New Jersey would serve no purpose. A ban on British imports, to start on 1 December, was unanimously voted on 27 September, but the export ban was delayed until the following autumn. The tobacco colonies insisted on the opportunity to sell next summer's crop, and a selective ban would have been unfair to others with goods to sell.

The logic of using the boycott weapon was a prior definition of the grievances to be redressed. On 14 October a Statement of Rights and Grievances listed all important colonial legislation since 1763, except the Declaratory Act. The latter could be ignored as being of no practical application, and a demand for its repeal would have alienated most sympathizers in Britain. But only six days later, when the crucial test was applied as to which measures were deemed important enough to justify a boycott, this list was reduced to little more than the 1774 legislation, together with all revenue measures. This was the demand in the Continental Association, which confirmed the boycott as an immediate ban from 1 December on all imports from Britain, and of British goods from elsewhere, and a ban from 10 September 1775 on all exports to Britain and her West Indies, if the specified Parliamentary legislation had not by then been repealed. [**DOCUMENT XI**] Local committees were to be established in counties and towns to enforce the boycott by ostracism of violators. Congress must have assumed that the mere threat of a trade recession would suffice to force Britain to back down, for the boycott could not have begun to bite before a reply was demanded. Congress had resolved to meet again as early as May 1775 unless the grievances had by then been redressed. Although the decisions of Congress were bad news for Britain, they were a moderate alternative to the military action already favoured by radical hotheads. Congress, indeed, had specifically warned Massachusetts not to provoke an armed conflict.

The challenge by Congress to Parliament's right to legislate at all for America was manifest, not only in the repeal demand but also in other ways: the deliberate failure to acknowledge Parliament's authority by any petition; and, after debates on the trade laws, the absence of any admission of Parliament's right to regulate colonial commerce. No concessions at all had been made. Nor had Congress made any constructive offer, even in the Address to the King which arrived in London on 17 December. Although respectful in tone, it simply requested a complete change of colonial policy.

The proceedings of the First Continental Congress had revealed the gulf between America and Britain. In the end, Congress had done all that the earlier local and provincial meetings had demanded, and more besides; for there had been little pressure in the summer for any Declaration of Rights. Not a single delegation had supported a suggestion by John Jay that Congress should offer compensation for the

Boston tea, and yet that step had been thought essential in Britain as a preliminary to reconciliation. Even the mere existence of Congress was regarded by most British politicians as a challenge to Parliament, and many thought it illegal. British opinion deemed the assemblies to be the only legitimate representative bodies in America, but the colonial majority now viewed Congress as the sole means of communicating with Britain, and separate decisions by assemblies were deplored as breaches of colonial solidarity.

Of more immediate significance than this potential constitutional argument was the misunderstanding by Congress of British opinion, and the American belief in the efficacy of a trade boycott. Although Congress had rejected military action, it had nevertheless deliberately challenged Britain. Congress was bluffing, confident that Britain would again yield ground, as in 1766 and 1770. This time Britain did not do so, and called the colonial bluff. The delegates at the Second Continental Congress in May 1775 might well have been faced with the choice of ignominious retreat from their 1774 demand or an armed conflict, which most of them did not want. As it happened, hostilities had accidentally already commenced. Otherwise, the War of Independence would have appeared more obviously what it was, the result of a political miscalculation by a Congress that had chosen to avoid a military conflict and yet blundered into one.

6. War and Independence

Accounts of the coming of the American Revolution often confuse the two distinct problems facing the British government at the beginning of 1775: the recovery of control of Massachusetts, and the attempt to find a compromise solution to the broader question of Britain's relationship with her colonies. Such reactions as the oft-quoted comment of George III to Lord North on 18 November 1774 that 'blows must decide whether they are to be subject to this country or independent' referred to the New England situation and did not imply the launching of a civil war.[1] That was not envisaged by the ministry as a policy option.

In January 1775 the cabinet decided to send military reinforcements to Gage in Massachusetts, and to riposte to the Continental Association by a ban on all colonial trade and fishing. But at the same time it approved in principle a proposal by Lord North that Britain should refrain from taxing colonies that made their own financial arrangements. Even if direct Parliamentary taxation of America was no longer possible — and there was a growing realization in Britain that this was the case — the North ministry never abandoned the aim of somehow obtaining money from the colonies. Its public propaganda maintained that policy attitude, notably in Samuel Johnson's pamphlet, *Taxation No Tyranny*. [**DOCUMENT XIII**]

It was to take some weeks to implement these decisions, but by the end of January the cabinet had settled on a force of over 3,000 men to be added to the 4,000 already in Boston. The instructions to Gage show clearly that the ministry was hoping to avert a civil war by prompt action, albeit with the risk of a brief armed clash.

Before the ministry introduced its policy in Parliament, Chatham seized the initiative. On 20 January he unsuccessfully proposed the withdrawal of the army from Boston. During the debate both opposition parties attacked the military coercion of America, Rockingham declaring that every American town to which troops were sent would become another Boston. Chatham then put forward a more comprehensive policy on 1 February. He would abandon Parliament's claim to complete sovereignty over America, although specifically reserving control of trade; concede the function of taxation to individual assemblies; and suspend all Parliamentary legislation of which complaint had been made in Congress's Declaration of Rights and Grievances. His proposal was heavily defeated. The plan conceded too much to be acceptable to Parliament, but not enough to earn the approval of Americans now renouncing Parliamentary supremacy altogether. The long-cherished view that if he had been Prime Minister he could have averted the break with America has no validity.

The ministry, aware of hostile feeling towards America in Parliament, deemed it politic to introduce first a condemnation of colonial behaviour, and measures to counter it, without any hint of concession. North set the tone on 2 February by a declaration that there had been a rebellion in Massachusetts, which would be met by the dispatch there of more soldiers and a ban on New England trade and fishing. He calculated that the average British tax burden per head of population was fifty times that in America, thus fuelling the anger of MPs. North also declared that Congress was challenging the legislative supremacy of Parliament. A majority of 304 to 105 for North's motion showed the strength of indignation against America at Westminster.

After North had followed this up by introducing a New England Trade and Fishery Bill, he felt able to announce on 20 February the concessionary part of the ministerial policy, what came to be known as his Conciliatory Proposition. Ignoring Congress, it stated that when any colony offered to pay for its civil government and its share of defence costs, Parliament would refrain from taxing that colony for revenue. This was to be North's idea of a permanent solution to the imperial crisis, and it became his war aim when America refused to accept it voluntarily. He commented that rejection by the colonists might lead to bloodshed, a hint to MPs that war was the alternative, and he tried to sell the plan to hardliners by holding out the prospect of a substantial revenue. He nevertheless failed to avert an attack by some of his own supporters on what they thought to be a disgraceful surrender to colonial resistance, a concession made before any American acknowledgement of Parliamentary supremacy. The episode demonstrated how much Parliamentary opinion limited the ministerial freedom of manœuvre. Suggestions by contemporary critics and subsequent historians that North should have enacted a more conciliatory policy in 1775, and thereby averted the American

Revolution, founder on the rock of political reality. No such proposal would have found support at Westminster. For a time on 20 February many thought that even North's modest plan would be rejected, but after the fury of the debate North's idea was approved by 274 votes to 88. [DOCUMENT XII] This part of the ministerial policy could be carried out without Parliamentary legislation, and it was put into effect at once by a circular letter sent on 3 March by the American Secretary, Dartmouth, to the colonial governors. The assemblies were to be left considerable discretion as to the method and amount of taxation, since they could decide the size of their own civil establishments.

Parliament was meanwhile concerned with the coercive legislation. On 6 March young Charles James Fox, already a leading member of the opposition, shrewdly argued that the ministry was using against the colonists the only Parliamentary power, that of regulating trade, that America accepted, and that they would therefore be driven to deny this also, as they had successively challenged those of taxation and legislation. Ministerial spokesmen, however, inferred from this progressive defiance that the colonies had always intended independence. On 9 March North proposed a second coercive measure, one to restrain the trade of six more colonies, since they had joined the Association. Three colonies were still excluded: New York, whose assembly had rejected the Congress decision; Georgia, which had not been represented there; and North Carolina, from which no bad news had yet arrived. Both Prohibitory Bills passed with little discussion.

There can be no doubt that the British political world was firmly behind this policy. On 10 April former Massachusetts Governor, Thomas Hutchinson, now in Britain, wrote to tell Gage that 'opposition is at an end . . . What expectations can America have from resistance?'[2] On 15 May a moderate petition from New York was rejected by the House of Commons because it questioned Parliament's right of taxation, and historian Edward Gibbon, himself a ministerial supporter, reflected that 'on America the Archangel Gabriel would not be heard'.[3]

Edmund Burke thought it incumbent on the opposition to do more than criticize. On 22 March he introduced a plan, on behalf of the Rockinghamite party, in what has become known as his 'Speech for Conciliation with the Colonies'. Burke, in contrast with both Chatham and North, disclaimed the idea of a colonial revenue as impractical and as unfair when Britain also controlled the American economy. He put forward a vision of an empire in which the colonies would be freely associated with Britain. 'Magnanimity in politics is not seldom the truest wisdom, and a great empire and little minds go ill together.'[4] Burke's famous oration delighted but failed to convince his audience. The ministerial response was that the colonial assemblies were as inferior to Parliament as borough corporations in England, and Lord George Germain contrived to use Burke's eloquence as a weapon against him: if he was not convinced by such a splendid speech, nothing could persuade him that his former opinion was wrong. The House of Commons rejected Burke's motion by 270 votes to 78.

The North ministry's American policy of early 1775 had for a long time a bad historical press. It apparently failed to avert the outbreak of civil war, and has seemed less forward-looking than the ideas of Chatham and Burke. These interpretations are misleading. The war began before the ministerial offer reached America, and the opposition proposals were also founded on the misconception that the quarrel was only about taxation. North's concession of the practice of internal taxation was a genuine attempt to solve the problem of imperial government as it was widely perceived in Britain.

Events in America at this time, had they been fully known in Britain, would have dispelled any optimism. All twelve colonies represented at the Continental Congress soon appointed delegates for the next meeting scheduled for May 1775. The assemblies of eleven of them, all but New York, endorsed the decisions of Congress. Even in that colony and in Georgia, who had not attended, there were some local moves to ban British goods. Towns and counties elected Committees to enforce the Continental Association, involving thousands of colonists in such direct action as the coercion or boycott of recalcitrant individuals. Although Congress had eschewed armed conflict, and hopes of a British climb-down deterred American preparations for fighting, other colonies besides Massachusetts took military precautions that winter. Inhabitants of both Rhode Island and New Hampshire looted arms from royal forts in December 1774, and several colonies, notably Virginia, began to raise militia. Supporters of the imperial status quo came to lose all influence, as when Joseph Galloway, long the political boss of Pennsylvania, fell from power there after the Assembly in March 1775 rejected his idea of a separate petition to the King. Everywhere during the winter of 1774–5 defiance of British rule was converted into the seizure of power by unofficial provincial Conventions, with effective local control being wielded by the Association Committees. Governor Josiah Martin of

North Carolina was barely exaggerating when he commented on 7 April that except for New York only the shadow of royal government remained, and that all trace of British rule would soon disappear. The New York Assembly had rejected the decisions of Congress, but its loyalist stance was undermined by unofficial action: the colony was to be represented at the second Congress by a delegation chosen by a popularly elected Convention.

In no colony was news of British policy more anxiously awaited than in Massachusetts. An armed truce prevailed there, for the local resistance leaders had been warned by Congress not to initiate a conflict, and the cautious Gage avoided any provocation until he received instructions on 14 April from Lord Dartmouth. Recognizing a call to action, he rejected the ministerial hint to arrest the colonial leaders, and decided to strike at their main arsenal at Concord, a half-day's march from Boston. It was this move, on 19 April, that precipitated fighting. Shots were exchanged at the village of Lexington between the British force and colonial militia, and subsequently at Concord and on the return march to Boston. Of 1,500 British soldiers involved that day, 73 were killed and 174 wounded: American losses were 49 dead and 39 injured.

News of Lexington did not reach London until 28 May, and the North ministry had meanwhile busied itself to prevent a war in New England. Gage was authorized to pardon at his discretion even those guilty of treason and rebellion, and was sent four regiments and three generals, William Howe, Henry Clinton, and John Burgoyne. Redoubled determination to subdue Massachusetts was the official reaction to news of the events of 19 April. George III commented that 'with firmness and perseverance America will be brought to submission'.[5] Not that his ministers needed exhortation. The cabinet's ideas soon included the use of Canadians and foreign soldiers, and of Red Indians when news came of colonial overtures to their tribes. The North ministry had accepted a state of war, and already envisaged a contest protracted into 1776.

It was equally obvious to most colonists that war had begun on 19 April. Boston was at once surrounded by thousands of militia, and the onset of widespread fighting in other colonies was prevented only by the absence of British army units. Outside the war area of New England, the weeks after Lexington witnessed the close of effective British rule. 'All legal authority and government seems to be drawing to an end here and that of congresses, conventions and committees establishing in their places'; so wrote Governor William Franklin of

New Jersey on 6 May.[6] Everywhere the story was of the coercion of loyalists and of the raising of local armed militia to ensure physical control of each colony for the new rebel institutions of government.

The Second Continental Congress met at Philadelphia from 10 May. The ostensible purpose was to seek reconciliation with Britain, and on 26 May a proposal to petition George III was carried after a long debate. But military preparations soon became the chief business after an initial reluctance by many delegates to accept the reality of a war situation had been overcome. On 14 June the decision was taken to create an army, and a former commander of the Virginia militia, George Washington, was appointed next day to head it, at the siege of Boston. Before he arrived there, the first battle of the war had taken place.

By mid-June the rebel noose had tightened around that town, the 17,000 militia force being more than twice the size of the British army. Gage nevertheless decided that he would break out on 18 June. His plan was leaked to the rebels, who forestalled it on 16 June by fortifying Breed's Hill, across the bay from Boston but commanding the town. This necessitated an immediate British response. In the ensuing battle next day, wrongly designated that of Bunker Hill, which lay behind, a British force of 2,200 men under General Howe cleared a rebel army twice its size from the encampment, but suffered almost a 50 per cent casualty rate, with 500 dead or soon to die. This bloody encounter deterred both sides from further conflict. Gage could see no useful purpose in attacking the enemy strongholds around Boston, and the lesson of Bunker Hill was that the British army would have to be moved out of Massachusetts.

Bunker Hill may have produced a military stalemate, but its political consequences were momentous. Reactions in America were both an intensification of the war effort and a hardening of political attitudes. On 30 June Congress approved 'Articles of War' to ensure army discipline, and, to resolve a manpower problem, recommended on 18 July that all fit men aged between sixteen and fifty should be embodied in the militia. By then Congress had approved, on 6 July, a declaration that Washington promulgated to his troops on 'the causes and necessity of their taking up arms'. This was simple propaganda, recapitulating alleged British aims and misdeeds, but care was taken to disclaim any motive of independence. [**DOCUMENT XIV**] Those Congress delegates anxious to tread that path were aware that premature disclosure of any such aim would be counterproductive, and they had, indeed, to accept one last gesture of reconciliation. John Dickinson, the 'Pennsylvania Farmer' of 1767 but now a moderate in the context of the 1775 situation, drafted the petition to the King that had earlier been agreed upon, and it was formally adopted on 8 July, being signed by all forty-eight delegates present. Known as the Olive Branch Petition, it made no complaints or demands, and expressed, in respectful language, a general desire for the restoration of harmony between Britain and America; but since Congress would not endorse any concession, it contained no specific proposals toward that end. [DOCUMENT XV]

The Congress not only failed to make a constructive move towards reconciliation; it also rejected the British initiative. Lord North's taxation proposal of 20 February was the most significant casualty on 19 April. The only three colonial assemblies that discussed it referred the decision to Congress, which on 31 July adopted a report drafted by radical Thomas Jefferson of Virginia. This claimed that Parliament was thereby usurping the rights of the colonies as to whether to vote money, for what purpose, and how much; for the British proposal was concerned only with the method of taxation. [DOCUMENT XVI] This unequivocal rejection of the policy that the North ministry was determined to impose on the colonies meant that there was no alternative to war. America would fight for the constitutional rights that Britain refused to acknowledge. But for many colonists this was not a decision for independence.

News of Bunker Hill reached London on 25 July. Public celebration of the victory concealed much private dismay at the casualty list. The cabinet accepted that an escalation of the conflict was inevitable, Lord North writing to George III next day that 'the war is now grown to such a height, that it must be treated as a foreign war'; but the final objective would still be the imposition on the colonies of his conciliatory proposal of 20 February.[7] Military planning was now for an army of at least 20,000 men to be assembled in America by the spring of 1776. Gage was replaced by Howe as army commander. New York was to become the centre of operations, but plans to evacuate Boston that autumn proved impossible to carry out, through lack of shipping and the onset of bad weather. Since home recruiting was a problem, recourse to foreign troops would be inevitable. There were high hopes in the summer of obtaining a Russian army, but in October a refusal came from Catherine II, and the ministry fell back on the traditional British resort to German mercenary soldiers.

Simultaneously with these military preparations, the ministry embarked on policy initiatives. The first step was a Proclamation of

Rebellion, and it was promulgated on 23 August, even though Congress was by then known to have voted a petition. [DOCUMENT XVII] The Olive Branch Petition was presented to the American Secretary, Dartmouth, on 1 September, but it was ignored by the ministry, no answer being given by the King. This behaviour played into the hands of those at Congress who favoured independence, but it did not mean that the cabinet had abandoned all thought of negotiation. Lord North was in fact coming round to the same idea that Dickinson and other promoters of the Petition had had in mind, a Peace Commission. Such a proposal had been vainly put forward by Dartmouth in cabinet during the previous winter. North now thought that Britain, with an army and a navy in America, would be able to enforce a satisfactory conclusion to the quarrel. A Peace Commission would negotiate about his Conciliatory Plan of February with individual colonies in turn after they had been forcibly cowed, if necessary: but it would not do so with Congress. Mindful of the Commons' reception of that proposal, North this time canvassed his hardline supporters before Parliament met.

North might entertain apprehensions about the intransigence of such MPs, but he had nothing to fear from any Parliamentary campaign on behalf of America that might be founded on either economic distress or political agitation. The impact of the American trade boycott was fortuitously more than balanced by a sudden expansion of the European market, with the onset of a period of peace in Eastern Europe. Despite the loss of the American market, British exports in 1775 were nearly 10 per cent higher than they had been in 1773. American Henry Cruger wrote from London to New York on 2 August that 'were it not for the newspapers, the people at large would hardly know there was a civil war in America . . . The manufacturers have full employment.'[8]

If no campaign to challenge ministerial policy could be based on complaints of a recession, neither was there any prospect of an upsurge of political sympathy for America in Britain. During the autumn of 1775 there was, on the contrary, a national demonstration of patriotic support for the King's government, which put into perspective the small radical movement in London. An important motive behind the Proclamation of Rebellion had been to encourage such a popular reaction. At least eighty Addresses supportive of government policy were organized during September and October, fifty-two of them from English and Scottish counties and boroughs. Only eight conciliatory petitions appeared, all from boroughs which had also sent

Addresses. During the next few months the balance was partly redressed, with sufficient petitions to demonstrate a substantial degree of opposition to the American War. Nevertheless, the overall totals were 126 Addresses to 26 petitions.

When Parliament met on 26 October 1775, the ministry began to reveal its policy, both denouncing the American behaviour as rebellion and hinting at a Peace Commission to negotiate from a position of strength. Before any move was made to implement this, Dartmouth informed North of his intention to resign, since his role as American Secretary had changed from that of conciliator to war minister. He was succeeded on 10 November by Lord George Germain, whose appointment injected a sense of vigour into the conduct of the war. The cabinet now decided to ask the rulers of Brunswick and Hesse-Cassel for the use of their soldiers in America. The plan was to send the Brunswick troops to Canada to counter the rebel attempt to conquer that colony, while the Hessians would reinforce Howe. Germain intended 1776 to be a positive campaign, to prevent discontent at home and to deter foreign intervention. He had himself long envisaged New York as the main British base, for it would split the rebel colonies.

Before the ministry produced its policy proposals, the indefatigable Edmund Burke put forward a Conciliation Bill on 16 November. It went beyond North's plan by, in effect, conceding to the colonies the right as well as the practice of taxation, and by a willingness to negotiate with a general meeting of colonial delegates. By way of a sweetener, he would first repeal the tea duty and the Massachusetts legislation of 1774. The ministry contended that such concessions would only encourage further resistance, and the House of Commons rejected Burke's Bill by 210 votes to 105. Four days later, opposition complaints that the ministry had no policy were answered when North introduced a comprehensive measure on 20 November. His intention was that the Peace Commissioners should be able to conduct genuine negotiations, and the aim of his so-called Prohibitory Act was to enable them to do so. That measure, the most misunderstood part of his American legislation, would therefore repeal the Boston Port Act and the two Acts of 1775 banning American trade, and replace them by a prohibition of all colonial trade. But, and this was the crucial point, the Peace Commission would be authorized to lift this ban on individual colonies if they came to terms, by which North meant acceptance of his Conciliatory Proposition. North's purpose was to give the Peace Commission a bargaining counter by this discretionary power. Much comment, contemporary and historical, has wrongly focused on the enforcement provisions of the trade ban, involving the forfeiture of colonial shipping and cargoes. The Parliamentary opposition was at such a low ebb that there was little discussion of the measure either on 20 November or during its subsequent passage before it received the royal assent on 22 December.

The policy decisions of the North ministry for 1776 had all been taken in principle before the end of 1775. There remained only their implementation: the provision of an army; the final decision on military strategy; and the appointment of a Peace Commission. Subsidy treaties were concluded early in 1776 for 12,000 Hessians and 5,000 Brunswickers. Military planning had to take account of the possibility that all Canada was in enemy hands, and about 10,000 men, half of them the Brunswickers, were to be sent there in the spring. For the main campaign, General Howe and Germain were at one in making New York the centre of operations. Howe was to take his Boston army there, reinforced by about 5,000 more British troops and all the Hessians. As events turned out, Britain had no choice but to evacuate the Massachusetts capital. On 4 March Washington suddenly deployed big guns on hills commanding Boston town and harbour. Howe realized that he could not remain there under danger of bombardment, but threatened to destroy the town unless he was permitted to leave unhindered. Washington bowed to political expediency and humanitarian principles, and thereby forfeited the chief military advantage of his coup. The British Dunkirk-like evacuation, on 17 March, was nevertheless a propaganda triumph for the rebels. Howe's force of 9,000 men sailed for Nova Scotia and remained there until June for recuperation, reorganization and reinforcement, before the projected New York campaign.

General Howe's brother, Lord Howe, one of Britain's most successful admirals of the century, had been offered the post of Peace Commissioner by Dartmouth. He then secured for himself the post of naval commander for America. Germain, however, would not accept him as sole Commissioner, and, after other nominations were rejected by the Admiral, his brother was made joint-Commissioner with him. There followed, from February until May, long arguments, both within the cabinet and between Germain and Lord Howe, as to what instructions the Howes were to be given. Germain in the end had to drop his demand for colonial acknowledgement of Parliamentary supremacy prior to negotiations, Howe insisting on the power to offer terms in order to procure a cessation of hostilities. His final instructions, dated 6 May, allowed the Commissioners to relieve any individual colony from the constraints of the Prohibitory Act as soon as it asked for terms. Howe boarded ship on 10 May, but the long delay destroyed whatever slight chance of success he might have had. Before he could commence his peace mission in America, colonial opinion had hardened into a decision for independence. This was not an unlucky coincidence. Those Americans who favoured a break with Britain took care to ensure that such a decision would be made before Howe's arrival. Military events in the colonies were eclipsed by political developments. Although the War of Independence is deemed to have begun on 19 April 1775, it was for the first year and more a phoney war. Little fighting took place outside the Boston area, and that mainly concerned the suppression of Loyalists in some southern colonies. The Declaration of Independence was to precede the commencement of full-scale hostilities.

The great public debate on independence began with the publication in January 1776 of Thomas Paine's pamphlet, *Common Sense*. Hitherto, the open quarrel with Britain had been over Parliament's claim to supremacy, and little challenge had been made to the sovereignty of George III. But it was becoming clear that the King was as much of a Parliamentarian as his ministers, and not at all disposed to play the role his American subjects wished of him, that of ruler of coequal parts of his dominions. The significance of *Common Sense* was the direct attack on the institution of monarchy and on George III, 'the Royal Brute of Great Britain', in person. [**DOCUMENT XVIII**] Within three months 120,000 copies had been sold, and the topic of independence dominated political discussion.

Congress debates and decisions reflected the changing mood in America. Perhaps the first straw in the wind was the quiet putting-aside on 13 February of a resolution explicitly denying independence as the aim. After a debate of some weeks, on 6 April Congress voted to open American ports to foreign shipping: that was an open challenge to the whole imperial system of trade regulation. On 10 May Congress formally recommended that individual colonies should establish their own governments, a virtual declaration of independence in itself and, to a large extent, merely a confirmation of what had already happened. Whatever official or loyalist correspondents may have misled the British government into thinking, the colonial movement towards independence was not a coup master-minded by a clique of radicals in the Congress, but a widespread popular response. Not only had the four New England colonies early trodden that path, but the three most southerly colonies, Georgia and the two Carolinas, had also already shown their support for the idea before the Virginia Convention on 15 May instructed its Congress delegates to propose independence. Richard Henry Lee did so on 7 June, but consideration was postponed until 1 July to give time for the five middle colonies to commit themselves. By that date, only the New York delegation was still forbidden to assent, and did not do so during the several days of debate before the Declaration of Independence was endorsed on 4 July; but a hastily convened New York Congress did vote approval five days later. The Declaration, drafted by Thomas Jefferson of Virginia, was a dishonest piece of propaganda. In order to justify the renunciation of George III's sovereignty, it blamed the King personally for the British policy decisions of the previous thirteen years that had hitherto correctly been attributed to his ministers and to Parliament. [**DOCUMENT XIX**] Much of posterity has thereby been deceived, even to this day!

Advocates of independence had just achieved their aim of a formal declaration in time to render the Peace Commission abortive. Lord Howe reached Halifax, Nova Scotia, on 23 June, only to find that General Howe had sailed for New York on 11 June. When Lord Howe arrived there on 12 July he was told by his brother that it would now be necessary to defeat the rebels before any negotiations could take place. The Declaration of Independence had put an end to the phoney war, and also the political debate within Britain as to whether coercion or conciliation should be the policy to pursue towards America.

The coming of the American Revolution was confused by various misconceptions and myths. Many colonists refused to accept that official policies enjoyed majority support in Britain, ascribing them to a tyrannical ministry and a corrupt Parliament. In Britain there flourished the conspiracy theory that the colonial resistance was master-minded by a few men intent from the first on independence. The most famous myth, both contemporary and historical, one that later formed part of the old 'Whig interpretation of history', was that America was the first line of defence of British liberty, as threatened by the wicked constitutional schemes of George III.

Such misunderstandings divert attention from the root cause of the American Revolution, the question of whether or not Parliament was the legislature for the British Empire. Public discussion of the constitutional relationship between Britain and her colonies was stimulated from 1763 because government measures increasingly took the form of Parliamentary legislation instead of executive action by the Crown. Hitherto Parliamentary sovereignty over Britain's overseas possessions had been tacitly assumed rather than frequently exercised or asserted. The colonial challenge during the Stamp Act Crisis led to the Declaratory Act of 1766, the first formal claim of full Parliamentary power over the colonies. It took some time for the colonists to dispute this outright. John Dickinson's *Farmer's Letters* of 1767–8, protesting against taxation altogether after the Townshend Duties, nevertheless pragmatically still placed the overall sovereignty of the British Empire in Parliament. The first practical exertion of the complete Parliamentary power claimed in 1766 occurred with the legislation of 1774. The Massachusetts Government Act signified the change of sovereign from King to Parliament by altering a charter granted by the Crown. That led to a direct colonial challenge to Parliament's power of legislation. It was an implicit demand for internal home rule under the Crown, and a claim quite incompatible with the maximum concession any British politician would make, that of the power of taxation. The King's support of Parliament led to the final break, but the belated denial of royal authority in the Declaration of Independence was an act of political expediency, not a constitutionally logical step. For throughout the earlier decade or so of controversy the sovereignty of the British Crown had been acknowledged in America.

Notes

[References are provided only for quotations]

Chapter 3. Crisis One: The Stamp Act

1. *The Bowdoin and Temple Papers* (Boston, Collections of Massachusetts Historical Society, 6th Series, 9, 1897), pp. 49–51.

Chapter 4. Crisis Two: The Townshend Duties

1. *Documents of the American Revolution, 1770–1783* (ed. K.G. Davies, 21 vols., Shannon, 1972–81), VI, 39–44.

Chapter 5. Crisis Three: The Boston Tea Party

1. *The Papers of Benjamin Franklin* (eds. L.W. Labaree, W.B. Willcox, 27 vols., New Haven, 1958–88. In progress), XXI, 152–3.

2. *Proceedings and Debates of the British Parliaments Respecting North America, 1754–1783* (eds. R.C. Simmons, P.D.G. Thomas, 6 vols., New York, 1982–6. In progress), IV, 89–112.

3. Ibid., IV, 402.

4. *The Correspondence of General Thomas Gage with the Secretaries of State and with the War Office and the Treasury, 1763–1775* (ed. C.E. Carter, 2 vols., New Haven, 1931–3), I, 357–60.

5. Ibid, I, 371.

Chapter 6. War and Independence

1. *The Correspondence of King George the Third from 1760 to December 1783* (ed. Sir John Fortescue, 6 vols., London, 1927–8), III, 157.

2. *The Diary and Letters of his Excellency Thomas Hutchinson, Esq.* (ed. P.O. Hutchinson, 2 vols., London, 1883–6), I, 435.

3. *The Letters of Edward Gibbon* (ed. J.E. Norton, 3 vols., London, 1956), II, 69.

4. *Proceedings and Debates*, V, 598–631.

5. *Reports of the Historical Manuscripts Commission, 13 Report, Appendix, Dartmouth MSS* (1892), pp. 501–2.

6. *Documents of the American Revolution*, IX, 126.

7. *Correspondence of George III*, III, 234–6.

8. Quoted in P.D.G. Thomas, *Tea Party to Independence: The Third Phase of the American Revolution, 1773–1776* (Oxford, 1991), p. 270.

Illustrative Documents

Sources, Acknowledgements and References

Documents I, III, VI, XI, XIV, XV, XVI, XVII and XIX appeared widely in the contemporary British and American press. Copies of these may be conveniently found in one or more of the collections of documents listed at the end of the Bibliography. Document II is extracted from the *Parliamentary Diaries of Nathaniel Ryder, 1764–1767*, edited by P.D.G. Thomas, *Camden Miscellany XXIII* (1969), with the permission of the Royal Historical Society. Document IV is from the Newcastle MSS in the British Library, by permission of the Trustees. Documents V and X constituted Parliamentary legislation, and statute references are given. Document VII is from the Camden (Pratt) MSS in the Kent County Record Office, by permission of that office. Document VIII was originally published in 1855 by the Massachusetts Historical Society. Documents IX and XII are press reports specific to the particular newspapers cited. Documents XIII and XVIII are extracted from individual pamphlets, as indicated.

DOCUMENT I   The Royal Proclamation of 7 October 1763

This was issued by the Privy Council, and concerned arrangements for Britain's new territories in North America, notably the creation of the new colonies of Quebec, East Florida, and West Florida. This extract established the remaining land as an Indian reservation.

And whereas it is just and reasonable, and essential to our interest and the security of our colonies, that the several nations or tribes of Indians with whom we are connected, and who live under our protection, should not be molested or disturbed in the possession of such parts of our dominions and territories as, not having been ceded to or purchased by us, are reserved to them, or any of them, as their hunting-grounds; we do therefore, with the advice of our Privy Council, declare it to be our royal will and pleasure, that no Governor or commander in chief, in any of our colonies of Quebec, East Florida, or West Florida, do presume, upon any pretence whatever, to grant warrants of survey, or pass any patents for lands beyond the bounds of their respective governments, as described in their commissions; as also that no Governor or commander in chief of our other colonies or plantations in America do presume for the present, and until our further pleasure be known, to grant warrants of survey or pass patents for any lands beyond the heads or sources of any of the rivers which fall into the Atlantic Ocean from the west or northwest; or upon any lands whatever, which, not having been ceded to or purchased by us, as aforesaid, are reserved to the said Indians, or any of them.

And we do further declare it to be our royal will and pleasure, for the present as aforesaid, to reserve under our sovereignty, protection, and dominion, for the use of the said Indians, all the land and territories not included within the limits of our said three new governments, or within the limits of the territory granted to the Hudson's Bay Company; as also all the land and territories lying to the westward of the sources of the rivers which fall into the sea from the west and northwest as aforesaid; and we do hereby strictly forbid, on pain of our displeasure, all our loving subjects from making any purchases or settlements whatever, or taking possession of any of the lands above reserved, without our special leave and license for that purpose first obtained.

And we do further strictly enjoin and require all persons whatever, who have either wilfully or inadvertently seated themselves upon any lands within the countries above described, or upon any other lands which, not having been ceded to or purchased by us, are still reserved to the said Indians as aforesaid, forthwith to remove themselves from such settlements.

DOCUMENT II   George Grenville's speech of 6 February 1765, introducing the Stamp Act resolutions

This is taken from the Parliamentary Diary of Nathaniel Ryder, an MP who took shorthand notes of some debates. They were not transcribed into longhand until the 1960s.

Grenville. Proposed taxing America from public motive. Private considerations of his own choice would have prevented him if they had been consulted. Wishes those who had gone before him had marked out a path to him which he might more easily follow. His conduct would then have been less liable to misconstruction.

The reason of the delaying the proposal to this year was to gain all possible information and to give Americans an opportunity of conveying information to this House, whose ears are always open to receive knowledge and to act to it. The officers of the revenue have done their duty in gaining all possible knowledge of the subject.

Objection, he said last year, that if the right of taxing was disputed he would not delay the question a moment. Wished now to avoid that question if possible, because he thinks no person can doubt it.

The objection of the colonies is from the general right of mankind not to be taxed but by their representatives. This goes to all laws in general. The Parliament of Great Britain virtually represents the whole Kingdom, not actually great trading towns. The merchants of London and the East India Company are not represented. Not a twentieth part of the people are actually represented.

All colonies are subject to the dominion of the mother country, whether they are a colony of the freest or the most absolute government. As to their charter, the Crown cannot exempt them by charter from paying taxes which are imposed by the whole legislature, but in fact the Crown has not done it . . .

The particular propriety of this mode of raising the tax. Objection, that this tax will produce disturbance and discontent and prevent improvement among the colonies. He has no motive, he can have no motive, for taxing a colony, but that of doing his duty. But as to this objection, when will the time come when enforcing a tax will not give discontent, if this tax does produce it after what we have done and suffered for America? And therefore if we reject this proposition now, we shall declare that we ought not to tax the colonies. And we need not declare after a year's time that we ought not, for then we cannot.

As to taxing themselves, how can so many colonies fix the proportion which they shall pay themselves? Supposing each county was to do this in England; supposing we were to assess the sum and let them tax themselves. What danger arises from this. While they remain dependent, they must be subject to our legislature. They have increased under former taxes and they will flourish under this. They have in many instances encroached and claimed powers and privileges inconsistent with their situation as colonies. If they are not subject to this burden of tax, they are not entitled to the privilege of Englishmen.

As to the propriety of this particular tax, the stamp tax takes in a great degree its proportion from the riches of the people. As in lawsuits and commercial contracts, it increases in proportion to the riches. No great number of officers, no unconstitutional authority in great Boards.

He has enquired from North America whether they objected to this particular species of tax and has not heard one gentleman propose any other. The tax in a great degree executes itself, as the instruments not stamped are null and void, and no person will trust that, especially as the case may be brought by appeal to this country.

DOCUMENT III Resolutions of the Stamp Act Congress, 19 October 1765

Twenty-seven delegates from nine colonies attended at New York.

The members of this Congress, sincerely devoted with the warmest sentiments of affection and duty to His Majesty's person and Government, inviolably attached to the present happy establishment of the Protestant succession, and with minds deeply impressed by a sense of the present and impending misfortunes of the British colonies on this continent; having considered as maturely as time will permit the circumstances of the said colonies, esteem it our indispensable duty to make the following declarations of our humble opinion respecting the most essential rights and liberties of the colonists, and of the grievances under which they labour, by reason of several late Acts of Parliament.

I.   That His Majesty's subjects in these colonies owe the same allegiance to the Crown of Great Britain that is owing from his subjects born within the realm, and all due subordination to that august body the Parliament of Great Britain.

II.   That His Majesty's liege subjects in these colonies are intitled to all the inherent rights and liberties of his natural born subjects within the kingdom of Great Britain.

III.   That it is inseparably essential to the freedom of a people, and the undoubted right of Englishmen, that no taxes be imposed on them but with their own consent, given personally or by their representatives.

IV.   That the people of these colonies are not, and from their local circumstances cannot be, represented in the House of Commons in Great Britain.

V.   That the only representatives of the people of these colonies are persons chosen therein by themselves, and that no taxes ever have been, or can be constitutionally imposed on them, but with their own consent, given personally or by their respective legislatures.

VI.   That all supplies to the Crown being free gifts of the people, it is unreasonable and inconsistent with the principles and spirit of the British Constitution, for the people of Great Britain to grant to His Majesty the property of the colonists.

VII. That trial by jury is the inherent and invaluable right of every British subject in these colonies.

VIII. That the late Act of Parliament, entitled *An Act for granting and applying certain stamp duties, and other duties, in the British colonies and plantations in America, etc.,* by imposing taxes on the inhabitants of these colonies; and the said Act, and several other Acts, by extending the jurisdiction of the courts of Admiralty beyond its ancient limits, have a manifest tendency to subvert the rights and liberties of the colonists.

IX.   That the duties imposed by several late Acts of Parliament, from the peculiar circumstances of these colonies, will be extremely burthensome and grievous; and from the scarcity of specie, the payment of them absolutely impracticable.

X.   That as the profits of the trade of these colonies ultimately center in Great Britain, to pay for the manufactures which they are obliged to take from thence, they eventually contribute very largely to all supplies granted there to the Crown.

XI.   That the restrictions imposed by several late Acts of Parliament on the trade of these colonies will render them unable to purchase the manufactures of Great Britain.

XII. That the increase, prosperity, and happiness of these colonies depend on the full and free enjoyments of their rights and liberties, and an intercourse with Great Britain mutually affectionate and advantageous.

XIII.   That it is the right of the British subjects in these
             colonies to petition the King or either House of Parlia-
             ment.

Lastly, That is the indispensable duty of these colonies to the best of
sovereigns, to the mother country, and to themselves, to endeavour by
a loyal and dutiful address to His Majesty, and humble applications
to both Houses of Parliament, to procure the repeal of the Act for
granting and applying certain stamp duties, of all clauses of any other
Acts of Parliament, whereby the jurisdiction of the Admiralty is
extended as aforesaid, and of the other late Acts for the restriction of
American commerce.

DOCUMENT IV   William Pitt's speech of 14 January 1766 on the Stamp Act

*The occasion was the debate on the Address at the opening of the Par-
liamentary session. This report is taken from a letter by James West MP
to the Duke of Newcastle, British Library, Additional MSS 32973, fos.
133–4. This version is more accurate than one published at the time in a
pamphlet on which many historians have relied.*

After Lord *Villiers* had moved the Address and Mr *T. Townshend*
very well seconded him, Mr *Seymour* spoke for enforcing the Stamp
Act and followed by Mr *Nugent* both in the same style with Lord
Sandwich in the House of Lords. Mr *Cooke* said the Act was illegal
and doubted the power of the Legislature of this country to tax the
Colonies. Mr *Stanley* answered him and was strong for enforcing the
Act and declared if he had produced only a pepper corn, the insisting
upon it was worth more than a million paid into the Exchequer as it
established the right which was of infinite consequence to this
country.

   Then Mr *Pitt* declared that this was the most important day he had
ever been present in, in Parliament and believed it was of greater
consequence than any day except when the Crown was settled. That
he came unconsulted and unconnected but he determined if alive to
come the first day if for fear of illness he should afterwards be
prevented. That the Act ought to be totally and absolutely repealed
as an erroneous policy, that no Treasury ever had thought of taxing
America in the most necessitous times, that the Parliament had no
power to enact an internal taxation in America, that it was not

represented here either virtually or otherwise. That to say America was virtually represented was a nonsensical absurdity, that the people here were taxed by a virtual representation, *that the best representation was that of counties, and that of great cities but as for the lesser boroughs he was confident their right to send representatives would in less than a century be amputated*; that he came in support only that American liberty was as dear to him as Englishmen. That this country was at its last gasp. That he thought there was a *point* whereby the whole might be happily concluded — first repeal the Stamp Act totally and absolutely then in a Committee regulate the whole of the American laws and deal with her as you would with a froward child or a wife;

> 'be to her faults a little blind,
> and I will to her virtues be very kind
> and clap the padlock on her mind.'

DOCUMENT V   The Declaratory Act, 18 March 1766

An Act for the better securing the dependency
of his Majesty's Dominions in America
Upon the Crown and Parliament of
Great Britain

WHEREAS *several of the houses of representatives in his Majesty's colonies and plantations in America, have of late, against law, claimed to themselves, or to the general assemblies of the same, the sole and exclusive right of imposing duties and taxes upon his Majesty's subjects in the said colonies and plantations; and have, in pursance of such claim, passed certain votes, resolutions, and orders, derogatory to the legislative authority of parliament, and inconsistent with the dependency of the said colonies and plantations upon the crown of* Great Britain: . . . be it declared . . . That the said colonies and plantations in *America* have been, are, and of right ought to be, subordinate unto, and dependent upon the imperial crown and parliament of *Great Britain*; and that the King's majesty, by and with the advice and consent of the lords spiritual and temporal, and commons of *Great Britain*, in parliament assembled, had, hath, and of right ought to have, full power and authority to make laws and statutes of sufficient force and validity to bind the colonies and people of *America*, subjects of the crown of *Great Britain*, in all cases whatsoever.

II. And be it further declared . . . That all resolutions, votes, orders, and proceedings, in any of the said colonies or plantations, whereby the power and authority of the parliament of *Great Britain*, to make laws and statutes as aforesaid, is denied, or drawn into question, are, and are hereby declared to be, utterly null and void to all intents and purposes whatsoever.

(Statutes at Large, XXVII, 19–20)

DOCUMENT VI   The Farmer's Letters, Letter Two, 7 December 1767

Written by Philadelphia lawyer, John Dickinson, this series of letters appeared in the American press after news of the Townshend Duties Act.

THERE IS another late act of Parliament which appears to me to be unconstitutional and as destructive to the liberty of these colonies as that mentioned in my last letter, that is, the act for granting the duties on paper, glass, etc.

The Parliament unquestionably possesses a legal authority to regulate the trade of Great Britain and all her colonies. Such an authority is essential to the relation between a mother country and her colonies; and necessary for the common good of all. He who considers these provinces as states distinct from the British Empire has very slender notions of justice or of their interests. We are but parts of a whole, and therefore there must exist a power somewhere to preside and preserve the connection in due order. This power is lodged in the Parliament; and we are as much dependent on Great Britain as a perfectly free people can be on another.

I have looked over every statute relating to these colonies from their first settlement to this time, and I find every one of them founded on this principle, till the Stamp Act administration. All before are calculated to regulate trade and preserve or promote a mutually beneficial intercourse between the several constituent parts of the empire. And though many of them imposed duties on trade, yet those duties were always imposed with design to restrain the commerce of one part that was injurious to another, and thus to promote the general welfare. The raising a revenue thereby was never intended . . . Never did the British Parliament, till the period above mentioned, think of imposing duties in America FOR THE PURPOSE OF RAISING A REVENUE . . .

Here we may observe an authority expressly claimed and exerted to impose duties on these colonies; not for the regulation of trade; not for the preservation or promotion of a mutually beneficial intercourse between the several constituent parts of the empire, heretofore the sole objects of Parliamentary institutions; but for the single purpose of levying money upon us.

This I call an innovation, and a most dangerous innovation. It may perhaps be objected that Great Britain has a right to lay what duties she pleases upon her exports, and it makes no difference to us whether they are paid here or there. To this I answer: These colonies require many things for their use which the laws of Great Britain prohibit them from getting anywhere but from her. Such are paper and glass.

That we may be legally bound to pay any general duties on these commodities relative to the regulation of trade is granted; but we being obliged by the laws to take from Great Britain, any special duties imposed on their exportation to us only with intention to raise a revenue from us only are as much taxes upon us as those imposed by the Stamp Act . . .

Here, then, my dear countrymen, ROUSE yourselves and behold the ruin hanging over your heads. If you ONCE admit that Great Britain may lay duties upon her exportations to us, for the purpose of levying money on us only, she then will have nothing to do but to lay those duties on the articles which she prohibits us to manufacture — and the tragedy of American liberty is finished . . . If Great Britain can order us to come to her for necessaries we want and can order us to pay what taxes she pleases before we take them away, or when we land them here, we are as abject slaves as France and Poland can show in wooden shoes and with uncombed hair.

DOCUMENT VII   The Cabinet Minute of 1 May 1769

In Grafton's handwriting. The additions 'N.B.' were made by the second Lord Camden, whose father had attended as Lord Chancellor. Lord Gower was Lord President.

At a meeting of the King's Servants at Lord Weymouth's Office

1 May 1769

Present

Lord Chancellor	Lord President
Duke of Grafton	Lord Granby
Lord Rochford	Lord Weymouth
Lord North	General Conway
	Lord Hillsborough

It is the unanimous opinion of the Lords present to submit to his Majesty as their advice that no measure should be taken which can any way derogate from the Legislative Authority of Great Britain over the Colonies. But that the Secretary of State in his correspondence and conversation be permitted to state it as the opinion of the King's servants that it is by no means the intention of Administration nor do they think it expedient or for the Interest of Great Britain or America to propose or consent to the laying any further Taxes upon America for the purpose of raising a Revenue, and that it is at present their Intention to propose in the next Session of Parliament to take off the Duties upon Paper, Glass and Colours imported into America upon consideration of such duties having been laid contrary to the true principles of commerce.

N.B. The Duke of Grafton tells me that 4 of these Lords had been desirous, but were outvoted, to have repealed the Duties on Tea also — viz. Lord Chancellor Camden, the Marquis of Granby, General Conway & the Duke of Grafton.

N.B. the above is written by the Duke of Grafton. Camden.

DOCUMENT VIII   The House of Commons debate of 5 March 1770 on the Townshend Duties

Extract from a letter of the Connecticut agent, William Samuel Johnson, to Governor J. Trumbull. Printed in Trumbull Papers, Collections of Massachusetts Historical Society, *fifth series, 9 [1855], pp. 421–3.*

At length the American Revenue Act has been debated in the House of Commons. Lord *North* moved yesterday for leave to bring in a Bill to repeal the duty upon three articles only, which he grounded upon the promise made by administration, in their circular letter, to propose it to Parliament, and upon the anti-commercial nature of those duties. The conduct of America, he said, had been such as in his opinion to prevent their going further, by their refusing to be content with this, by their entering into and continuing their combinations against the trade of this country, which he called insolent, unwarrantable, and illegal, and such as Parliament must not yield to, nor could without giving up all authority over the colonies. He insisted that the preamble to the Act and the duty on tea must be retained, as a mark of the supremacy of Parliament, and an efficient declaration of their right to govern the colonies. He said it was also an *operative duty*, and fairly within our old distinction between internal and external taxes, the latter of which we had admitted they might impose. This was a port duty, not an internal tax. That our new distinction between taxes for raising a revenue and duties for regulation of trade, was too vague to be a line of conduct, and would never answer any practical purpose; that whatever duties were imposed, they might call them regulations of trade, while we should insist they were for the purpose of revenue, and the consequence would be they could impose none to which America would agree. He expatiated upon the infractions of the agreements by the people of Boston, and various other circumstances there, (of which he appeared to have the most minute and circumstantial intelligence,) as tending to evince that those agreements would soon come to nothing; upon the impossibility of our manufacturing for the supply of any considerable part of our necessities, and their ability to check us if it should ever become necessary; and concluded that our necessities and want of union would open the trade, and, with the attention of government, secure the dependence of the colonies. He admitted that New York and Pennsylvania had kept strictly to their agreements, but imagined they would soon give way, as they found them disregarded by others, etc., etc.

The *Lord Mayor* of London [William Beckford] urged the repeal of the whole Act, upon the ground of justice to the East India Company, and upon commercial principles; but found much fault with the claims and principles advanced in a pamphlet lately published by the Boston merchants. Governor *Pownall* pursued the same points in a very sensible speech, demonstrated the ruinous, alarming situation of the trade, from the course of exchange, the Petition of the merchants, and many other circumstances; urged the ability of America to manufacture, the progress she had already made, the ill policy of pursuing such measures as tended to push her into them, and produce at the same time disaffection in the colonies; went into many other collateral points relative to America, and concluded very warmly on the subject of the military.

General *Mackay*, lately returned from Boston, told a long, stupid story of his observations in that country, very little to the advantage of Boston, and much of it, I believe, very ill-founded. Mr *Grenville* repeated his old opinions of American affairs, insisted upon the want of plan in the conduct of administration, and, till there was some plan or other, said he would have no concern in the business: if there was any honor to be acquired by what they were doing, he wished for none of it; if there was any blame to be incurred, he would bear no part of it; and refused to give his vote upon this occasion. He was seconded in his general notions by Mr *Wedderburn*, and some others. Lord *North* was supported by several ministerial speakers, who repeated and enforced his ideas. Lord *Barrington*, and some of his friends, expatiated (though not in very harsh terms) upon the ill conduct of the colonies, and upon that ground opposed the repeal of any part of the Act. General *Conway*, Sir *William Meredith*, and Colonel *Barré* spoke for the repeal of the whole, the two latter, especially, extremely well. Barré had some fine strokes. Upon the whole, it was not a very lively debate, and finally, about twelve o'clock, it was carried against the amendment (which had been proposed by Mr Pownall, to include the tea with the other articles), by 204 to 142; several, I believe, having followed the example of Mr Grenville, and voted on neither side. The Bill will therefore be brought in only for the repeal of the other duties, exclusive of the tea.

DOCUMENT IX   The Boston Tea Party, 16 December 1773

Report in the London Evening Post, *21 January 1774, 'from the Boston Gazette'.*

Boston, Dec. 20. On Tuesday last the body of the people of this, and all the adjacent towns, and others from the distance of twenty miles, assembled at the Old South Meeting House, to enquire the reason of the delay in sending the ship *Dartmouth* with the East India tea back to London; and having found that the owner had not taken the necessary steps for that purpose, they enjoined him at his peril, to demand of the Collector of Customs, a clearance for the ship, and appointed a committee of ten to see it performed; after which they adjourned to the Thursday following, ten o'clock. They then met, and being informed by Mr Rotch that a clearance was refused him, they enjoined him immediately to enter a protest, and apply to the Governor for a passport by the Castle, and adjourned again till three o'clock for the same day. At which time they again met, and after waiting till near sun-set, Mr Rotch came in, and informed them that he had accordingly entered his protest, and waited on the Governor for a pass; but his Excellency told him he could not, consistent with his duty, grant it until his vessel was qualified. The people finding all their efforts to preserve the property of the East India Company, and return it safely to London, frustrated by the tea consignees, the Collector of the Customs, and the Governor of the Province, dissolved their meeting.

But, behold, what followed! A number of resolute men (dressed like Mohawks or Indians) determined to do all in their power to save their country from the ruin which their enemies had plotted, in less than four hours emptied every chest of tea on board the three ships commanded by the Captains Hall, Bruce, and Coffin, amounting to 342 chests, into the sea, without the least damage done to the ships, or any other property. The masters and owners are well pleased that their ships are thus cleared; and the people are almost universally congratulating each other on this happy event.

DOCUMENT X   The Boston Port Act, 31 March 1774

Whereas dangerous commotions and insurrections have been fomented and raised in the town of Boston, in the province of Massachusetts Bay in New England, by divers ill-affected persons, to the subversion of his Majesty's government and to the utter destruction of the public peace and good order of the said town; in which commotions and insurrections certain valuable cargoes of teas, being the property of the East India Company and on board certain vessels lying within the bay or harbour of Boston, were seized and destroyed; and whereas, in the present condition of the said town and harbour the commerce of his Majesty's subjects cannot be safely carried on there, nor the customs payable to his Majesty duly collected; and it is therefore expedient that the officers of his Majesty's customs should be forthwith removed from the said town: . . . be it enacted . . . [that trade there is unlawful from 1 June 1774] . . .

IV. Provided always, that nothing in this Act contained shall extend, or be construed to extend to any military or other stores for his Majesty's use, or to the ships or vessels whereupon the same shall be laden, which shall be commissioned by, and in the immediate pay of his Majesty, his heirs or successors; nor to any fuel or victual brought coastwise from any part of the continent of America, for the necessary use and sustenance of the inhabitants of the said town of Boston . . .

X. Provided also, and it is hereby declared and enacted, that nothing herein contained shall extend, or be construed, to enable his Majesty to appoint such port, harbour, creeks, quays, wharfs, places, or officers, in the said town of Boston, or in the said bay or islands, until it shall sufficiently appear to his Majesty that full satisfaction has been made by or on behalf of the inhabitants of the said town of Boston to the United Company of Merchants of England Trading to the East Indies, for the damage sustained by the said company by the destruction of their goods sent to the said town of Boston, on board certain ships or vessels as aforesaid . . .

(Statutes at Large, XXX, 336–41.)

DOCUMENT XI   The Continental Association, 20 October 1774

Issued by the First Continental Congress at Philadelphia.

We, his Majesty's most loyal subjects, the delegates of the several colonies of New Hampshire, Massachusetts Bay, Rhode Island, Connecticut, New York, New Jersey, Pennsylvania, the three lower counties of Newcastle, Kent and Sussex on Delaware, Maryland, Virginia, North Carolina, and South Carolina, deputed to represent them in a continental congress, held in the city of Philadelphia, on the 5th day of September, 1774, avowing our allegiance to his Majesty, our affection and regard for our fellow-subjects in Great Britain and elsewhere, affected with the deepest anxiety and most alarming apprehensions, at those grievances and distresses, with which his Majesty's American subjects are oppressed; and having taken under our most serious deliberation the state of the whole continent, find that the present unhappy situation of our affairs is occasioned by a ruinous system of colony administration, adopted by the British ministry about the year 1763, evidently calculated for enslaving these colonies, and with them, the British Empire. In prosecution of which system various Acts of Parliament have been passed for raising a revenue in America, for depriving the American subjects, in many instances, of the constitutional trial by jury, exposing their lives to danger, by directing a new and illegal trial beyond the seas, for crimes alleged to have been commited in America; and in prosecution of the same system, several late, cruel and oppressive Acts have been passed, respecting the town of Boston and the Massachusetts Bay, and also an Act for extending the province of Quebec, so as to border on the western frontiers of these colonies, establishing an arbitrary government therein, and discouraging the settlement of British subjects in that wide extended country; thus, by the influence of civil principles and ancient prejudices, to dispose the inhabitants to act with hostility against the free Protestant colonies, whenever a wicked ministry shall choose so to direct them.

To obtain redress of these grievances which threaten destruction to the lives, liberty, and property of his Majesty's subjects, in North America, we are of opinion that a non-importation, non-consumption, and non-exportation agreement, faithfully adhered to, will prove the most speedy, effectual, and peaceable measure: and therefore, we do, for ourselves, and the inhabitants of the several colonies whom we represent, firmly agree and associate, under the sacred ties of virtue, honour and love of our country, as follows:

1. That from and after the first day of December next, we will not import into British America, from Great Britain or Ireland, any goods, wares or merchandise whatsoever, or from any other place, any such goods, wares, or merchandise, as shall have been exported from Great Britain or Ireland; nor will we, after that day, import any East India tea from any part of the world; nor any molasses, syrups, paneles, coffee, or pimento, from the British plantations or from Dominica; nor wines from Madeira, or the Western Islands; nor foreign indigo . . .

4. The earnest desire we have not to injure our fellow-subjects in Great Britain, Ireland, or the West Indies, induces us to suspend a non-exportation until the tenth day of September, 1775; at which time, if the said Acts and parts of Acts of the British Parliament hereinafter mentioned are not repealed, we will not, directly or indirectly, export any merchandise or commodity whatsoever to Great Britain, Ireland or the West Indies, except rice to Europe . . .

11. That a committee be chosen in every county, city, and town by those who are qualified to vote for representatives in the legislature, whose business it shall be attentively to observe the conduct of all persons touching this Association; and when it shall be made to appear to the satisfaction of a majority of any such committee that any

person within the limits of their appointment has violated this Association, that such majority do forthwith cause the truth of the case to be published in the gazette; to the end that all such foes to the rights of British America may be publicly known, and universally condemned as the enemies of American liberty; and thenceforth we respectively will break off all dealings with him or her . . .

DOCUMENT XII Lord North's Conciliatory Proposition, 20 February 1775

Newspapers were by now publishing reports of Parliamentary debates. This account of Lord North's speech is taken from the London Chronicle *for 25 February 1775.*

Grievances, he observed, can only be settled by a dutiful application to government; and when subjects apply in that manner, it is right and fit to grant whatever indulgence is necessary. The exercise of the right of taxing every part of the British dominions, must by no means be given up; the proposition I have now made only states upon what ground it may be suspended: and though it may be asked, whether it be possible for Parliament to come to any resolution on that subject, while we are sending fleets and armies in order to lay the trade of the colonies under restrictions; yet I think it best at the outset to let them know what we expect, and to learn whether they mean to dispute the whole of our authority or not. And though I admit it is not worth while to spend the lives of his Majesty's subjects in levying a trifling tax upon them; it is certainly worth every exertion to secure their allegiance, and to enforce the supreme legislative authority of this country. Their congress was certainly an illegal assembly; for they are separate states, independent on each other, and have no connection but in their relation to Great Britain. Our army and navy establishment we all know are necessarily encreased on their account, and for their protection; they ought therefore to contribute their just proportion to that expence, subject to the disposal of Parliament. I will never depart from the proper exercise of that right, when they refuse to contribute voluntarily; which if they do, I shall think it right to suspend the exercise of our power to tax them here, except for the regulation of commerce. Very often the best method of regulating commerce is by taxation. But to remove every objection that other taxes may be raised upon them under the colour of regulations on commerce; I mean that the produce of such duties shall be applied to the particular use of that province where they are levied. Parliament cannot divest itself of the right of taxation in every part of the empire, because it may become necessary to demand assistance and supply from every corner of it. The colonies complain that Parliament is ignorant of their true state; but this is only a specious pretence: let them first tax themselves, and then it will be seen whether suspension of taxation accompanies their contribution. The proposition I have now the honour of offering to the Committee, is no dishonourable concession, because, in the present condition of things, the mother country, in the moment of victory over them, would demand no more; we are not treating with enemies, nor wishing to take any advantage of them; but only to settle a dispute between subject and subject, on a lasting foundation. It may likewise be objected, that America pays enough already; but I beg leave to remind the Committee, that the subjects of Britain now pay £1,800,000 yearly, to discharge the interest on the debt contracted last war, our conquests in which, left the colonies in a state of ease and security. Again it may be said, will you treat with rebels? I am not inclined to treat, but to demand; nor do I mean in the least to suspend our military operations by sea and land, until they submit to the laws. Whether any colony will come in on these terms I know not; but I am sure it is both just and humane to give them the option. If one of them consents, a link of the great chain is broken. If not, which possibly may be the case, and that they shall make no offer whatever; or none that we can with any propriety accept; this conduct of theirs, must convince men of justice and humanity at home, that our dispute with America is not about modes of taxation, but that they have deeper views, and mean to throw off all dependence upon this country, and to get rid of every controul of the legislature. I hope at least this will not lessen our unanimity at home, though I never expect to see that unanimity so much to be wished for, on a matter of this importance.

Lord North then proposed the following resolution, which was carried by 274 votes to 88 after a long debate. This text is from the official Commons Journals, *XXXV, 161:*

That it is the opinion of this Committee that when the Governor, Council, and Assembly, or General Court, of any of his Majesty's provinces or colonies in America, shall propose to make provision, according to the condition, circumstances and situation of such province or colony, for contributing their proportion to the common defence (such proportion to be raised under the authority of the General Court or General Assembly of such Province or Colony, and disposeable by Parliament) and shall engage to make provision also for the support of the civil government and the administration of justice in such Province or Colony, it will be proper if such proposal shall be approved by his Majesty and the two Houses of Parliament, or for so long as such provision shall be made accordingly, to forbear in respect of such Province or Colony to levy any duty, tax, or assessment, or to impose any further duty, tax, or assessment, except only such duties as it may be expedient to continue to levy or to impose for the regulation of commerce, the net produce of the duties last mentioned to be carried to the account of such Province or Colony respectively.

DOCUMENT XIII *Taxation No Tyranny*, 8 March 1775

The author of this pro-government pamphlet was the famous man of letters, Dr Samuel Johnson.

But terrours and pity are not the only means by which the taxation of the *Americans* is opposed. There are those who profess to use them only as auxiliaries to reason and justice, who tell us that to tax the Colonies is usurpation and oppression, an invasion of natural and legal rights, and a violation of those principles which support the Constitution of *English* Government.

This question is of great importance. That the *Americans* are able to bear taxation, is indubitable; that their refusal may be overruled, is highly probable; but power is no sufficient evidence of truth. Let us examine our own claim, and the objections of the recusants, with caution proportioned to the event of the decision, which must convict one part of robbery, or the other of rebellion.

A tax is a payment exacted by authority from part of the community for the benefit of the whole. From whom, and in what proportion, such payment shall be required, and to what uses it shall be applied, those only are to judge to whom Government is intrusted. In the *British* Dominion taxes are apportioned, levied, and appropriated by the states assembled in Parliament.

Of every Empire, all the subordinate communities are liable to taxation, because they all share the benefits of Government, and therefore ought all to furnish their proportion of the expense.

This the *Americans* have never openly denied. That it is their duty to pay the cost of their own safety, they seem to admit; nor do they refuse their contribution to the exigencies, whatever they may be, of the *British* Empire; but they make this participation of the publick burden a duty of very uncertain extent and imperfect obligation — a duty, temporary, occasional, and elective, of which they reserve to themselves the right of settling the degree, the time, and the duration of judging when it may be required and when it has been performed.

They allow to the supreme power nothing more than the liberty of notifying to them its demands or its necessities. Of this notification, they profess to think for themselves, how far it shall influence their counsels, and of the necessities alleged, how far they shall endeavour to relieve them. They assume the exclusive power of settling not only the mode but the quantity of this payment. They are ready to co-operate with all the other Dominions of the King; but they will co-operate by no means which they do not like, and at no greater charge than they are willing to bear.

This claim, wild as it may seem — this claim, which supposes dominion without authority, and subjects without subordination, has found among the libertines of policy many clamorous and hardy vindicators. The laws of nature, the rights of humanity, the faith of Charters, the danger of liberty, the encroachments of usurpation, have been thundered in our ears, sometimes by interested faction, and sometimes by honest stupidity.

DOCUMENT XIV Declaration of the causes and necessity for taking up arms, 6 July 1775

Written jointly by Thomas Jefferson and John Dickinson, this was published by General George Washington when he took command of the American army besieging Boston.

But why should we enumerate our injuries in detail? By one statute it is declared that Parliament can 'of right make laws to bind US IN ALL CASES WHATSOEVER'. What is to defend us against so enormous, so unlimited a power? Not a single man of those who assume it is chosen by us; or is subject to our control or influence; but, on the contrary, they are all of them exempt from the operation of such laws, and an American revenue, if not diverted from the ostensible purposes for which it is raised, would actually lighten their own burdens in proportion as they increase ours. We saw the misery to which such despotism would reduce us. We for ten years incessantly and ineffectually besieged the throne as supplicants; we reasoned, we remonstrated with Parliament, in the most mild and decent language. But administration, sensible that we should regard these oppressive measures as freemen ought to do, sent over fleets and armies to enforce them. The indignation of the Americans was roused, it is true; but it was the indignation of a virtuous, loyal, and affectionate people. A congress of delegates from the united colonies was assembled at Philadelphia on the fifth day of last September. We resolved again to offer an humble and dutiful petition to the king, and also addressed our fellow-subjects of Great Britain. We have pursued every temperate, every respectful measure: we have even proceeded to break off our commercial intercourse with our fellow-subjects, as the last peacable admonition, that our attachment to no nation upon earth should supplant our attachment to liberty.

We are reduced to the alternative of choosing an unconditional submission to the tyranny of irritated ministers, or resistance by force. The latter is our choice. We have counted the cost of this contest and find nothing so dreadful as voluntary slavery. Honour, justice, and humanity forbid us tamely to surrender that freedom which we received from our gallant ancestors, and which our innocent posterity have a right to receive from us. We cannot endure the infamy and guilt of resigning succeeding generations to that wretchedness which inevitably awaits them, if we basely entail heredi-tary bondage upon them.

Our cause is just. Our union is perfect. Our internal resources are great, and, if necessary, foreign assistance is undoubtedly attainable. We gratefully acknowledge, as signal instances of the Divine favour towards us, that his Providence would not permit us to be called into this severe controversy, until we were grown up to our present strength, had been previously exercised in warlike operation, and possessed of the means of defending ourselves. With hearts fortified with these animating reflections, we most solemnly, before God and the world, declare, that, exerting the utmost energy of those powers which our beneficent Creator hath graciously bestowed upon us, the arms we have been compelled by our enemies to assume, we will in defiance of every hazard, with unabating firmness and perseverance, employ for the preservation of our liberties; being with one mind resolved to die free men rather than live slaves.

Lest this declaration should disquiet the minds of our friends and fellow-subjects in any part of the empire, we assure them that we mean not to dissolve that union which has so long and so happily subsisted between us, and which we sincerely wish to see restored. Necessity has not yet driven us into that desperate measure, or induced us to excite any other nation to war against them. We have not raised armies with ambitious designs of separating from Great Britain, and establishing independent states. We fight not for glory or for conquest. We exhibit to mankind the remarkable spectacle of a people attacked by unprovoked enemies, without any imputation or even suspicion of offence. They boast of their privileges and civilization, and yet proffer no milder conditions than servitude or death.

In our own native land, in defence of the freedom that is our birthright, and which we ever enjoyed till the late violation of it, for the protection of our property, acquired solely by the honest industry of our forefathers and ourselves, against violence actually offered, we have taken up arms. We shall lay them down when hostilities shall cease on the part of the aggressors, and all danger of their being renewed shall be removed, and not before.

DOCUMENT XV The Olive Branch Petition, 8 July 1775

This was written by John Dickinson, and voted unanimously by the Second Continental Congress.

Attached to your Majesty's person, family, and government, with all devotion that principle and affection can inspire, connected with Great Britain by the strongest ties that can unite societies, and deploring every event that tends in any degree to weaken them, we solemnly assure your Majesty that we not only most ardently desire the former harmony between her and these colonies may be restored, but that a concord may be established between them upon so firm a basis as to perpetuate its blessings, uninterrupted by any future dissensions, to succeeding generations in both countries, and to transmit your Majesty's name to posterity, adorned with that signal and lasting glory that has attended the memory of those illustrious personages whose virtues and abilities have extricated states from dangerous convulsions, and, by securing happiness to others, have erected the most noble and durable monuments to their own fame.

We beg leave further to assure your Majesty that notwithstanding the sufferings of your loyal colonists during the course of the present controversy, our breasts retain too tender a regard for the kingdom from which we derive our origin to request such a reconciliation as might in any manner be inconsistent with her dignity or her welfare. These, related as we are to her honour and duty as well as inclination, induce us to support and advance; and the apprehensions that now oppress our hearts with unspeakable grief being once removed, your Majesty will find your faithful subjects on this continent ready and willing at all times, as they ever have been, with their lives and fortunes to assert and maintain the rights and interests of your Majesty, and of our mother country.

We, therefore, beseech your Majesty that your royal authority and influence may be graciously interposed to procure us relief from our afflicting fears and jealousies, occasioned by the system before mentioned, and to settle peace through every part of your dominions, with all humility submitting to your Majesty's wise consideration whether it may not be expedient for facilitating those important purposes, that your Majesty be pleased to direct some mode by which the united applications of your faithful colonists to the throne, in pursuance of their common councils, may be improved into a happy and permanent reconciliation; and that, in the mean time, measures may be taken for preventing the further destruction of the lives of your Majesty's subjects; and that such statutes as more immediately distress any of your Majesty's colonies may be repealed.

For by such arrangements as your Majesty's wisdom can form for collecting the united sense of your American people, we are convinced your Majesty would receive such satisfactory proofs of the disposition of the colonists towards their sovereign and parent state that the wished for opportunity would soon be restored to them of evincing the sincerity of their professions by every testimony of devotion becoming the most dutiful subjects, and the most affectionate colonists.

That your Majesty may enjoy a long and prosperous reign, and that your descendants may govern your dominions with honour to themselves and happiness to their subjects, is our sincere and fervent prayer.

DOCUMENT XVI   The rejection by Congress of Lord North's Conciliatory Proposition, 31 July 1775

This answer was primarily the work of Thomas Jefferson. The other members of the drafting Committee were John Adams, Benjamin Franklin, and Richard Henry Lee.

The Congress took the said resolution into consideration, and are thereupon of opinion,

That the colonies of America are entitled to the sole and exclusive privilege of giving and granting their own money; that this involves a right of deliberating whether they will make any gift, for what purposes it shall be made, and what shall be its amount; and that it is a high breach of this privilege for any body of men, extraneous to their constitutions, to prescribe the purposes for which money shall be levied on them, to take to themselves the authority of judging of their conditions, circumstances, and situations, and of determining the amount of the contribution to be levied.

That as the colonies possess a right of appropriating their gifts, so are they entitled at all times to inquire into their application, to see that they be not wasted among the venal and corrupt for the purpose of undermining the civil rights of the givers, nor yet be diverted to the support of standing armies, inconsistent with their freedom and subversive of their quiet. To propose, therefore, as this resolution does, that the moneys given by the colonies shall be subject to the disposal of Parliament alone, is to propose that they shall relinquish this right of inquiry and put it in the power of others to render their gifts ruinous, in proportion as they are liberal.

That this privilege of giving or of withholding our moneys is an important barrier against the undue exertion of prerogative, which, if left altogether without control may be exercised to our great oppression; and all history shows how efficacious is its intercession for redress of grievances and re-establishment of rights, and how improvident it would be to part with so powerful a mediator.

We are of opinion that the proposition contained in this resolution is unreasonable and insidious: unreasonable, because if we declare we accede to it, we declare without reservation we will purchase the favour of Parliament, not knowing at the same time at what price they will please to estimate their favour. It is insidious because individual colonies, having bid and bidden again till they find the avidity of the seller too great for all their powers to satisfy; are then to return into opposition, divided from their sister colonies whom the minister will have previously detached by a grant of easier terms, or by an artful procrastination of a definitive answer.

That the suspension of the exercise of their pretended power of taxation being expressly made commensurate with the continuance of our gifts, these must be perpetual to make that so. Whereas no experience has shown that a gift of perpetual revenue secures a perpetual return of duty or of kind disposition. On the contrary, the Parliament itself, wisely attentive to this observation, are in the established practice of granting their supplies from year to year only.

DOCUMENT XVII   The Royal Proclamation of Rebellion, 23 August 1775

This was drafted by the North ministry, and issued through the Privy Council.

Whereas many of our subjects in divers parts of our colonies and plantations in North America, misled by dangerous and ill-designing men, and forgetting the allegiance which they owe to the power that has protected and sustained them, after various disorderly acts committed in disturbance of the public peace, to the obstruction of lawful commerce and to the oppression of our loyal subjects carrying on the same, have at length proceeded to an open and avowed rebellion by arraying themselves in hostile manner to withstand the execution of the law, and traitorously preparing, ordering, and levying war against us; and whereas there is reason to apprehend that such rebellion hath been much promoted and encouraged by the traitorous correspondence, counsels, and comfort of divers wicked and desperate persons within this realm; to the end therefore that none of our subjects may neglect or violate their duty through ignorance thereof, or through any doubt of the protection which the law will afford to their loyalty and zeal; we have thought fit, by and with the advice of our Privy Council, to issue this our royal proclamation, hereby declaring that not only all our officers, civil and military, are obliged to exert their utmost endeavours to suppress such rebellion and to bring the traitors to justice; but that all our subjects of this realm and the dominions thereunto belonging are bound by law to be aiding and assisting in the suppression of such rebellion, and to disclose and make known all traitorous conspiracies and attempts against us, our Crown, and dignity; and we do accordingly strictly charge and command all our officers, as well civil as military, and all other our obedient and loyal subjects, to use their utmost endeavours to withstand and suppress such rebellion, and to disclose and make known all treasons and traitorous conspiracies which they shall know to be against us, our Crown and dignity; and for that purpose, that they transmit to one of our principal secretaries of state, or other proper officer, due and full information of all persons who shall be found carrying on correspondence with, or in any manner or degree aiding or abetting the persons now in open arms and rebellion against our government within any of our colonies and plantations in North America, in order to bring to condign punishment the authors, perpetrators and abettors of such traitorous designs.

Given at our court at St James the twenty-third day of August, one thousand seven hundred and seventy-five, in the fifteenth year of our reign.

DOCUMENT XVIII   *Common Sense*, 10 January 1776

Published anonymously in Philadelphia. The author was Thomas Paine, an English Quaker who emigrated to America in 1774.

That the crown is this overbearing part in the English constitution, needs not be mentioned, and that it derives its whole consequence merely from being the giver of places and pensions, is self-evident; wherefore, though we have been wise enough to shut and lock a door against absolute monarchy, we at the same time have been foolish enough to put the crown in possession of the key . . .

To the evil of monarchy we have added that of hereditary succession: and as the first is a degradation and lessening of ourselves, so the second, claimed as a matter of right, is an insult and an imposition on posterity. For all men being originally equals, no *one* by birth could have a right to set up his own family in perpetual preference to all others for ever, and though himself might deserve *some* decent degree of honours of his contemporaries, yet his descendants might be far too unworthy to inherit them. One of the strongest *natural* proofs of the folly of hereditary rights in kings, is, that nature disapproves it, otherwise she would not so frequently turn it into ridicule by giving mankind an *Ass for a Lion* . . .

England, since the conquest, hath known some few good monarchs, but groaned beneath a much larger number of bad ones; yet no man in his senses can say that their claim under William the Conqueror is a very honourable one. A French bastard landing with an armed banditti, and establishing himself king of England against the consent of the natives, is in plain terms a very paltry rascally original. It certainly hath no divinity in it. However, it is needless to spend much time in exposing the folly of hereditary right; if there are any so weak as to believe it, let them promiscuously worship the ass and the lion, and welcome. I shall neither copy their humility, nor disturb their devotion . . .

But where, say some, is the King of America? I'll tell you, Friend, he reigns above, and doth not make havoc of mankind like the Royal Brute of Great Britain. Yet that we may not appear to be defective even in earthly honours, let a day be solemnly set apart for proclaiming the Charter; let it be brought forth placed on the Divine Law, the word of God; let a crown be placed thereon, by which the world may know, that so far as we approve of monarchy, that in America THE LAW IS KING.

For as in absolute governments the King is law, so in free countries the law *ought* to be King; and there ought to be no other. But lest any ill use should afterwards arise, let the Crown at the conclusion of the ceremony be demolished, and scattered among the People whose right it is . . .

O ye that love mankind! Ye that dare oppose not only the tyranny, but the tyrant, stand forth! Every spot of the old world is over-run with oppression. Freedom hath been hunted round the globe. Asia and Africa have long expelled her. Europe regards her like a stranger, and England hath given her warning to depart. O! receive the fugitive, and prepare in time an asylum for mankind.

DOCUMENT XIX   The Declaration of Independence, 4 July 1776

This was voted by the Second Continental Congress. The author was Thomas Jefferson.

WHEN in the Course of human Events, it becomes necessary for one People to dissolve the Political Bands which have connected them with another, and to assume among the Powers of the Earth, the separate and equal Station to which the Laws of Nature and of Nature's God entitle them, a decent Respect to the Opinions of Mankind requires that they should declare the causes which impel them to the Separation.

WE hold these Truths to be self-evident, that all Men are created equal, that they are endowed by their Creator with certain unalienable Rights, that among these are Life, Liberty, and the Pursuit of Happiness — That to secure these Rights, Governments are instituted among Men, deriving their just Powers from the Consent of the Governed, that whenever any Form of Government becomes destructive of these Ends, it is the Right of the People to alter or to abolish it, and to institute new Government, laying its Foundation on such Principles, and organizing its Powers in such Form, as to them shall seem most likely to effect their Safety and Happiness. Prudence, indeed, will dictate that Governments long established should not be changed for light and transient Causes; and accordingly all Experience hath shewn, that Mankind are more disposed to suffer, while Evils are sufferable, than to right themselves by abolishing the Forms to which they are accustomed. But when a long Train of Abuses and Usurpations, pursuing invariably the same Object, evinces a Design to reduce them under absolute Despotism, it is their Right, it is their Duty, to throw off such Government, and to provide new Guards for their future Security. Such has been the patient Sufferance of these Colonies; and such is now the Necessity which constrains them to alter their former Systems of Government. The History of the present King of Great-Britain is a History of repeated Injuries and Usurpations, all having in direct Object the Establishment of an absolute Tyranny over these States. To prove this, let Facts be submitted to a candid World.

HE has refused his Assent to Laws, the most wholesome and necessary for the public Good.

HE has forbidden his Governors to pass Laws of immediate and pressing Importance, unless suspended in their Operation till his Assent should be obtained; and when so suspended, he has utterly neglected to attend to them.

HE has refused to pass other Laws for the Accommodation of large Districts of People, unless those People would relinquish the Right of Representation in the Legislature, a Right inestimable to them, and formidable to Tyrants only.

HE has called together Legislative Bodies at Places unusual, uncomfortable, and distant from the Depository of their public Records, for the sole Purpose of fatiguing them into Compliance with his Measures.

HE has dissolved Representative Houses repeatedly, for opposing with manly Firmness his Invasions on the Rights of the People.

HE has refused for a long Time, after such Dissolutions, to cause others to be elected; whereby the Legislative Powers, incapable of Annihilation, have returned to the People at large for their exercise; the State remaining in the mean time exposed to all the Dangers of Invasion from without, and Convulsions within.

HE has endeavoured to prevent the Population of these States; for that Purpose obstructing the Laws for Naturalization of Foreigners; refusing to pass others to encourage their Migrations hither, and raising the Conditions of new Appropriations of Lands.

HE has obstructed the Administration of Justice, by refusing his Assent to Laws for establishing Judiciary Powers.

HE has made Judges dependent on his Will alone, for the Tenure of their Offices, and the Amount and Payment of their Salaries.

HE has erected a Multitude of new Offices, and sent hither Swarms of Officers to harass our People, and eat out their Substance.

HE has kept among us, in Times of Peace, Standing Armies, without the consent of our Legislatures.

HE has affected to render the Military independent of and superior to the Civil Power.

HE has combined with others to subject us to a Jurisdiction foreign to our Constitution, and unacknowledged by our Laws; giving his Assent to their Acts of pretended Legislation:

FOR quartering large Bodies of Armed Troops among us:

FOR protecting them, by a mock Trial, from Punishment for any Murders which they should commit on the Inhabitants of these States:

FOR cutting off our Trade with all Parts of the World:

FOR imposing Taxes on us without our Consent:

FOR depriving us, in many Cases, of the Benefits of Trial by Jury:

FOR transporting us beyond Seas to be tried for pretended Offences:

FOR abolishing the free System of English Laws in a neighbouring Province, establishing therein an arbitrary Government, and enlarging its Boundaries, so as to render it at once an Example and fit Instrument for introducing the same absolute Rule into these Colonies:

FOR taking away our Charters, abolishing our most valuable Laws, and altering fundamentally the Forms of our Governments:

FOR suspending our own Legislatures, and declaring themselves invested with Power to legislate for us in all Cases whatsoever.

HE has abdicated Government here, by declaring us out of his Protection and waging War against us.

HE has plundered our Seas, ravaged our Coasts, burnt our Towns, and destroyed the Lives of our People.

HE is, at this Time, transporting large Armies of foreign Mercenaries to compleat the Works of Death, Desolation, and Tyranny, already begun with circumstances of Cruelty and Perfidy, scarcely paralleled in the most barbarous Ages, and totally unworthy the Head of a civilized Nation.

HE has constrained our fellow Citizens taken Captive on the high Seas to bear Arms against their Country, to become the Executioners of their Friends and Brethren, or to fall themselves by their Hands.

HE has excited domestic Insurrections amongst us, and has endeavoured to bring on the Inhabitants of our Frontiers, the merciless Indian Savages, whose known Rule of Warfare, is an undistinguished Destruction, of all Ages, Sexes and Conditions.

IN every stage of these Oppressions we have Petitioned for Redress in the most humble Terms: Our repeated Petitions have been answered only by repeated Injury. A Prince, whose Character is thus marked by every act which may define a Tyrant, is unfit to be the Ruler of a free People.

NOR have we been wanting in Attentions to our British Brethren. We have warned them from Time to Time of Attempts by their Legislature to extend an unwarrantable Jurisdiction over us. We have reminded them of the Circumstances of our Emigration and Settlement here. We have appealed to their native Justice and Magnanimity, and we have conjured them by the Ties of our common Kindred to disavow these Usurpations, which, would inevitably interrupt our Connections and Correspondence. They too have been deaf to the Voice of Justice and of Consanguinity. We must, therefore, acquiesce in the Necessity, which denounces our Separation, and hold them, as we hold the rest of Mankind, Enemies in War, in Peace, Friends.

WE, therefore, the Representatives of the UNITED STATES OF AMERICA, in GENERAL CONGRESS, Assembled, appealing to the Supreme Judge of the World for the Rectitude of our Intentions, do, in the Name, and by Authority of the good People of these Colonies, solemnly Publish and Declare, That these United Colonies are, and of Right ought to be, FREE AND INDEPENDENT STATES; that they are absolved from all Allegiance to the British Crown, and that all political Connection between them and the State of Great Britain, is and ought to be totally dissolved; and that as

FREE AND INDEPENDENT STATES, they have full Power to levy War, conclude Peace, contract Alliances, establish Commerce, and to do all other Acts and Things which INDEPENDENT STATES may of right do. And for the support of this Declaration, with a firm Reliance on the Protection of divine Providence, we mutually pledge to each other our Lives, our Fortunes, and our sacred Honor.

Signed by
ORDER AND IN BEHALF *of the* CONGRESS,
JOHN HANCOCK, PRESIDENT.

ATTEST.
CHARLES THOMSON, SECRETARY.

Bibliography

The literature on the American Revolution is so vast that this suggested reading must be seen as a preliminary guide. Of one-volume general surveys, the most useful, though dated by much new work since 1975, is Ian. R. Christie and Benjamin W. Labaree, *Empire or Independence, 1760–1776: A British-American Dialogue on the Coming of the American Revolution* (Oxford, Phaidon Press, 1976). Representative of the imperial school is L.H. Gipson, *The Coming of the Revolution, 1763–1775* (London, Hamish Hamilton, 1954), as Merrill Jensen, *The Founding of a Nation: A History of the American Revolution, 1763–1776* (New York, Oxford University Press, 1968), is of the Progressive tradition. An anticipated definitive work that proved disappointing was Robert Middlekauff, *The Glorious Cause: The American Revolution, 1763–1789* (New York, Oxford University Press, 1982). Vitiated by American bias and ignorant of Britain, it is a colourful narrative, but nothing more. By contrast, Robert W. Tucker and David C. Hendrickson, *The Fall of the First British Empire: Origins of the War of American Independence* (Baltimore, John Hopkins University Press, 1982), is not a narrative at all, but an analysis of historical writing.

Coverage of the British side of the Revolution was for long thin and patchy. C.R. Ritcheson essayed a pioneer general survey, *British Politics and the American Revolution* (Norman, University of Oklahoma Press, 1954). Paul Langford's *The First Rockingham Administration, 1765–1766* (London, Oxford University Press, 1973) analysed that ministry's reaction to the Stamp Act Crisis. Bernard Donoughue, in *British Politics and the American Revolution: The Path to War, 1773–75* (London, Macmillan, 1964), studied British policy-making between the Boston Tea Party and Lexington. Peter D.G. Thomas has recently completed a three-volume study of the formulation of British policy between 1763 and 1776: *British Politics and the Stamp Act Crisis: The First Phase of the American Revolution, 1763–1767* (Oxford, Clarendon Press, 1975); *The Townshend Duties Crisis:*

The Second Phase of the American Revolution, 1767–1773 (Oxford, Clarendon Press, 1987); *Tea Party to Independence: The Third Phase of the American Revolution, 1773–1776* (Oxford, Clarendon Press, 1991). Little new was added by John L. Bullion, *A Great and Necessary Measure: George Grenville and the Genesis of the Stamp Act, 1763–1765* (Columbia, University of Missouri Press, 1982). John Derry, *English Politics and the American Revolution* (London, J.M. Dent, 1976), considered attitudes rather than policies. Keith Perry's brief *British Politics and the American Revolution* (London, Macmillan, 1990), is erratic and error-prone.

Biographies of George III include John Brooke, *King George III* (London, Constable, 1972), and Stanley Ayling, *George the Third* (London, Collins, 1972); see also Peter D.G. Thomas, 'George III and the American Revolution', *History*, 70 (1985), 16–31. There are modern biographies of four of the five Prime Ministers: Philip Lawson, *George Grenville: A Political Life* (Oxford, Clarendon Press, 1984); Ross J.S. Hoffman, *The Marquis: A Study of Lord Rockingham, 1730–1782* (New York, Fordham University Press, 1973); Stanley Ayling, *The Elder Pitt* (London, Collins, 1976); and Peter D.G. Thomas, *Lord North* (London, Allen Lane, 1976). There is no biography of Grafton, nor of the first American Secretary, Lord Hillsborough. For his successors, see B.D. Bargar, *Lord Dartmouth and the American Revolution* (Columbia, University of South Carolina Press, 1965), and Gerald Saxon Brown, *The American Secretary: The Colonial Policy of Lord George Germain, 1775–1778* (Ann Arbor, The University of Michigan Press, 1963). See also Sir Lewis Namier and John Brooke, *Charles Townshend* (London, Macmillan, 1964), and Cornelius P. Forster, *The Uncontrolled Chancellor: Charles Townshend and His American Policy* (Providence, The Rhode Island Bicentennial Foundation, 1978).

Two studies of the colonial agents in Britain are Michael G. Kammen, *A Rope of Sand: The Colonial Agents, British Politics and the American Revolution* (Ithaca, Cornell University Press, 1968), and Jack M. Sosin, *Agents and Merchants: British Colonial Policy and the Origins of the American Revolution, 1763–1775* (Lincoln, University of Nebraska Press, 1965). For political and popular criticism of British policy, see Colin Bonwick, *English Radicals and the American Revolution* (Chapel Hill, University of North Carolina Press, 1977); John Sainsbury, *Disaffected Patriots: London Supporters of Revolutionary America, 1769–1782* (Montreal, McGill-Queen's University Press, 1987); and James E. Bradley, *Popular Politics and the American*

Revolution in England: Petitions, the Crown, and Public Opinion (Macon, Mercer University Press, 1986). An older general study is Dora Mae Clark, *British Opinion and the American Revolution* (New York, Russell and Russell, 1966 reprint of 1930 edition). Also dated is Fred J. Hinkhouse, *The Preliminaries of the American Revolution as seen in the English Press, 1763–1775* (New York, Columbia University Press, 1926). Cartoons may be found in Peter D.G. Thomas, *The American Revolution* (Cambridge, Chadwyck-Healey, 1986).

On the American side of the Revolution, the gradual alienation of the colonists has been traced in several scholarly monographs. Bernard Knollenberg, *Origin of the American Revolution, 1759–1766* (New York, Macmillan, 1960), puts the worst possible interpretations on British policy. Edmund S. and Helen M. Morgan, *The Stamp Act Crisis: Prologue to Revolution* (Chapel Hill, University of North Carolina Press, 1953), is both a classic and a standard account of that first clash. Pauline Maier, *From Resistance to Revolution: Colonial Radicals and the Development of American Opposition to Britain, 1765–1776* (London, Routledge and Kegan Paul, 1973), continues the story to independence. Hiller B. Zobel, *The Boston Massacre* (New York, Norton, 1971), is definitive, as is Benjamin Woods Labaree, *The Boston Tea Party* (New York, Oxford University Press, 1964). David Ammerman, *In the Common Cause: American Response to the Coercive Acts of 1774* (Charlottesville, University of Virginia Press, 1974), is now the book to read on the First Continental Congress. On the final break with Britain, see Jerrilyn Greene Marston, *King and Congress: The Transfer of Political Legitimacy, 1774–1776* (Princeton, Princeton University Press, 1987), and Garry Wills, *Inventing America: Jefferson's Declaration of Independence* (New York, Doubleday and Company, 1978).

On the economic background, O.M. Dickerson, *The Navigation Acts and the American Revolution* (Philadelphia, University of Pennsylvania Press, 1951), is a general introduction, but the picture of compliance with the trade laws is contradicted by Thomas C. Barrow, *Trade and Empire: The British Customs Service in Colonial America, 1660–1775* (Cambridge, Mass., Harvard University Press, 1967). A.M. Schlesinger, *The Colonial Merchants and the American Revolution, 1763–1776* (New York, Columbia University Press, 1918), is still valuable for information, but a modern correction is J.W. Tyler, *Smugglers and Patriots: Boston Merchants and the Advent of the American Revolution* (Boston, Northeastern University Press, 1986). Most modern surveys discount economic oppression as a significant factor in the coming of the Revolution, and pay little attention also to religious motivation. The latter topic is explored in Alan Heimert, *Religion and the American Mind from the Great Awakening to the Revolution* (Cambridge, Mass., Harvard University Press, 1966). For unfounded colonial fears that an episcopate would be imposed on America, see Carl Bridenbaugh, *Mitre and Sceptre: Transatlantic Faiths, Ideals, Personalities and Politics, 1689–1775* (New York, Oxford University Press, 1962). But the pulpit was one vehicle for propaganda, as is demonstrated by Philip Davidson, *Propaganda and the American Revolution, 1763–1783* (Chapel Hill, University of North Carolina Press, 1941). For an introduction to the wider intellectual background, see Bernard Bailyn, *The Ideological Origins of the American Revolution* (Cambridge, Mass., Harvard University Press, 1967).

On the frontier question, J.M. Sosin's *Whitehall and the Wilderness; The Middle West in British Colonial Policy, 1760–1775* (Lincoln, University of Nebraska Press, 1961), needs to be read in conjunction with important articles by P.D. Marshall: 'Sir William Johnson and the Treaty of Fort Stanwix, 1768', *Journal of American Studies*, 1 (1967), 149–79; and 'Colonial protest and imperial retrenchment: Indian policy 1764–1768', ibid., 5 (1971), 1–17. For the military background, and its political implications, see John W. Shy, *Towards Lexington: The Role of the British Army in the Coming of the American Revolution* (Princeton, Princeton University Press, 1965); and the biography by John R. Alden of its commander from 1763 to 1775, *General Gage in America* (Baton Rouge, Louisiana State University Press, 1948).

Losers tend to be overlooked by historians, but in recent decades the Loyalists have received much belated attention. The modern pioneer work was W.H. Nelson, *The American Tory* (London, Oxford University Press, 1961), and much detail may be found in R.M. Calhoon, *The Loyalists in Revolutionary America* (New York, Bruce Jovanovich, 1973). Bernard Bailyn highlighted *The Ordeal of Thomas Hutchinson* (Cambridge, Mass., Harvard University Press, 1974).

Much of the most illuminating writing on the Revolution has indeed been in the form of biographies. The most active campaigner against Britain is studied in John C. Miller's *Sam Adams: Pioneer in Propaganda* (Stanford, Stanford University Press, 1936). On Benjamin Franklin, the classic biography is Carl Van Doren, *Benjamin Franklin* (London, Putnam, 1939); the most recent is Esmond Wright, *Franklin of Philadelphia* (Cambridge, Mass.,

Harvard University Press, 1986); and also useful is Cecil B. Currey, *Road to Revolution: Benjamin Franklin in England, 1765–1775* (New York, Anchor Books, 1968). George Washington is of little importance in this period, but of Douglas Southall Freeman's unfinished biography the relevant (third) volume is *Planter and Patriot, 1758–1775* (London, Eyre and Spottiswoode, 1951). Likewise for Thomas Jefferson, see the first volume of the massive life by Dumas Malone, *Jefferson the Virginian* (London, Eyre and Spottiswoode, 1948). Dated but readable is Catherine Drinker Bowen, *John Adams and the American Revolution* (Boston, Little, Brown and Co., 1950). Short biographies, all published by English Universities Press, London, are Max Beloff, *Thomas Jefferson and American Democracy* (1948); Esmond Wright, *Washington and the American Revolution* (1957); and Esmond Wright, *Benjamin Franklin and American Independence* (1966).

For those who wish to pursue the subject further through contemporary sources, the fullest general collection of documents is Merrill Jensen's *English Historical Documents: IX, American Colonial Documents to 1776* (London, Eyre and Spottiswoode, 1955, reprinted 1969). Also useful are Samuel Eliot Morison (ed.), *Sources and Documents illustrating the American Revolution, 1764–1788* (New York, Oxford University Press, 1923, and subsequent editions); Max Beloff (ed.), *The Debate on the American Revolution, 1761–1783* (London, Nicholas Kaye, 1949); and Richard B. Morris (ed.), *The American Revolution, 1763–1783: A Bicentennial Collection* (New York, Harper and Row, 1970).

Index